DREAMS DON'T DIE

DREAMS DON'T DIE

THE STORY OF A MAN
ON A MISSION
TO INSPIRE A GENERATION
OF DREAMERS

IZEK SHOMOF

with **DON YAEGER**

Forefront
BOOKS

Published by Forefront Books.
Distributed by Simon & Schuster.

Library of Congress Control Number: 2023914002

Print ISBN: 978-1-63763-241-3
E-BOOK ISBN: 978-1-63763-242-0

Cover Design by Bruce Gore, Gore Studio, Inc.
Interior Design by Mary Susan Oleson, BLU Design Concepts

DEDICATION

To MY WIFE, ALINE, whose love, support, and understanding have made all of this possible. Thank you for being by my side throughout all these years and helping to create what we both accomplished.

CONTENTS

CHAPTER 1

JUSTICE

My journey from the back streets of Tel Aviv to the lofty heights of Beverly Hills has been filled with diversions. At every point, I had to make a decision about which fork in the road to take. Which one would lead me in the right direction? It's always been my way of life to do the right thing, but sometimes you don't realize you've done the right thing until long after you've done it. And sometimes you don't realize how life-changing a single event was.

When I was sixteen, I opened the first of my three restaurants in Los Angeles. The third restaurant I opened was a burger joint at the corner of Seventh Street and South Los Angeles Street. Today it's a street corner like hundreds of others in Los Angeles, bustling with small businesses and reflecting the hopes and dreams of people like me who are searching for their own piece of the American Dream. There's a parking garage and some shops, including a small restaurant, where my burger joint used to be. My burger joint stood where the entrance to the parking garage is today. To me, it was the entrance to a new life. That's where I got started and where I learned the lessons that set me on the road to success.

One day as I walked past the alley behind my burger joint, something caught my eye. I knew there was a homeless guy who pretty much lived in the alley with his few belongings. He was a white guy, probably in his forties. But to a teenager like me, he seemed much older. I don't think I'd ever seen his face clearly, though. He was a faceless, nameless guy, like so many other homeless individuals in Los Angeles, and I never gave him a second thought until that day—the day that changed my life.

All of a sudden, the owner of the clothing store next to my burger joint ran up to the homeless guy and pepper-sprayed him in his face. He just maced him without any warning. Of course, the homeless guy went crazy from the pain. Shocked and confused, he started screaming. His face and his eyes were red and burning, and tears were rolling down his face.

I was just a kid, but I knew this wasn't right. I couldn't believe what I'd just seen, and it stopped me in my tracks. I was horrified. Without thinking, I went up to the store owner and asked, "What the hell did you do? Why did you do that? How could you do such a thing?" The store owner didn't say a word and just looked at me in a weird way before skulking back to his shop like nothing had happened.

This all happened in the space of a few moments, and the air was still thick with the spicy sharpness of the pepper spray. As the homeless guy sat on the ground, rubbing his eyes and trying to breathe, I grabbed the hose I kept at the back of my restaurant. My own eyes had started to water, and I could feel the irritation in my nose and throat, but I knelt down and washed the man's face and rinsed out his eyes until the worst of his suffering had stopped.

I don't really know where I found the strength or the courage to stand up to the store owner, but all these years later I can look back on that day and realize my actions sprang from a feeling somewhere deep within me—from something innate that I had learned about right and wrong and justice. So many thoughts went through my head, but I'd seen bullying and injustice before from customers at my parents' restaurant in Tel Aviv, and I had learned that the only way to deal with it was to confront it. Perhaps that was the birthplace of my courage.

I could have been like so many others and shrugged off the store owner's actions. I could have said, "Well, you know, that's what homeless guys get." But I believe that when you see someone who is hurting, you come to their aid. At the very least, I had to stand up for the homeless man, because it's likely that few people ever had. I had the ability to help him, and I couldn't let him suffer.

After I got the homeless guy cleaned up, I went back to work in my restaurant. I checked on him a few hours later. He was doing a little better, and eventually he went on his way, perhaps not even thinking much more about the incident. It may not have been the first time someone had tried to get rid of him like that. Perhaps he'd been maced before, even by that same store owner, and perhaps he was used to being abused by people who hoped he'd move on and become someone else's problem.

I never knew the man's name, and I don't remember ever seeing him again, so it's likely he got my neighbor's message. But that terrible incident on that particular day made a great impact on my life.

* * *

The idea that there were homeless people in America was a shock to me. It blew my mind. I came to America—the richest and most progressive country in the world—from Israel when I was fourteen years old. Israel was a brand-new country back then, literally just twenty-five years old at the time, not much older than me.

I had never seen homelessness in Israel. I didn't even know what being homeless meant, so it was shocking to see people in the United States begging on the streets, digging through trash cans for scraps of food, and sleeping in the alleys. It was especially shocking to a young guy like me who could go home to his parents' house, sleep in his own bed, take a shower, and use the toilet whenever he wanted. I could always get something to eat when I was hungry and relax by watching TV in a comfortable living room. I was always safe. So when I saw a homeless person with minimal possessions sitting on the sidewalk or sleeping in an alleyway, I found it shocking and disturbing.

JUSTICE

Like most other cultures around the world, Israelis have a great tradition of respecting the family—and because Israel is a small country and families tend to stay in the same place, it is rare to see a homeless Israeli or Jewish person. Their families would always support them and not allow them to become homeless. Even my own cousin Levi—who was one of the first armed bank robbers in Israel and later a drug lord in the US— was never rejected by our family and was always welcomed back home, no matter what he had done. His life was not necessarily something to be proud of, but he was family, and he's part of our history.

* * *

The pepper spray incident with the homeless man was the first time I'd had any type of personal interaction with the homeless on the streets in Los Angeles, other than being shocked by their very existence. I'd always noticed them, but I had never talked to them or touched them until that moment. I remember thinking, *For heaven's sake, do we live in a Third World country?* For the first time, I saw the face of inhumanity, and it touched me. Ever since then, I've been trying to treat the homeless like family. It has been one of the driving forces in my life. I live comfortably, and I've built a real estate business in Los Angeles, but I've never forgotten how sick it made me feel to witness one man attack another just because he was homeless.

It is because of this that I have invested so much in the Life

13

Rebuilding Center that promises to revolutionize the way Los Angeles deals with the homeless. Standing up for a homeless guy when I was sixteen is the same as what I'm doing now, all these years later—except now I can make a much bigger difference. It's a continuous cycle, connecting what happened when I was young to searching for the right path for the rest of my life.

I've often wondered where the justice is in attacking a man simply because he is homeless or a different color or a different religion. Sure, homeless people are not always exactly easy for property owners or business owners to have around. They may urinate on the property, they might smell bad, and their actions can sometimes chase away customers, so I understand how the homeless guy could have bothered the store owner. But I've never understood how it reached the point of violence. The homeless are still human beings. They're our brothers and sisters, and they deserve our respect and love.

I'm not a religious person, but in the Torah (the first five books of the Old Testament), there is a Hebrew word, *tzedek*, that translates as *justice*. To make the point clearly, it's repeated as *tzedek, tzedek*, because it implies double-checking—thinking twice and making sure you're doing the right thing or searching for the correct solution. Pepper-spraying the homeless man in the face was *not* the right thing to do, and it was not seeking justice for the so-called sin of being homeless and sleeping in the alley. The store owner did not think twice. If he had done so, he may have found a compassionate way to deal with his frustration and anger.

JUSTICE

Understanding *tzedek* is perhaps the most valuable lesson in my life. In fact, *tzedek* has been my guiding principle in all that I do, and it's actually embedded into my heart. I have a tattoo over my heart with the words *tzedek, tzedek, tirdof,* meaning "fairness and justice." The point is that if you're talking to a friend or doing business with someone and you get into an argument with them, you may think you're correct. They may think they're correct. The beauty here is that if you stop and think again, you may realize you're wrong. By living out the principle of *tzedek,* you can always follow what is right, even if it's the opposite of what you originally thought and even if it doesn't benefit you. *Tzedek, tzedek, tirdof*—think about it a second time. It's a great message, and it's one of the most important pieces of advice I've passed on to my children.

Perhaps I would have reached the same conclusion at some other point in my life, but that incident when I was sixteen opened my eyes to the world and showed me a way forward that I have never looked back from or regretted. Every success I have had, from businesses to family, stems from the realization that I must stop and think clearly in order to choose the right direction whenever I come to a fork in the road. Choose wisely.

CHAPTER 2

TEL AVIV

I spent the first fourteen years of my life in Tel Aviv, Israel. I was born in the city on July 28, 1959, only a little more than eleven years after the modern State of Israel was formed in 1948. Israel, like me, was developing its own unique identity, and we were growing up together.

My parents came to Israel in 1933 from the southern part of the Soviet Union, around the cities of Bukhara and Tashkent, but it appears that past generations may have lived closer to Moscow at various times.

Sara, my mother, was eight years old and Hanan, my father, was eleven when their families arrived in Jerusalem. Of course, Israel did not exist back then. It was known as Palestine, but everyone knew this was where the Promised Land was, and Jews were coming from all over because they hoped Israel would one day become a state. Like thousands of others, my grandparents must have felt such euphoria upon reaching the Promised Land, even though the land was occupied by both

Jews and Arabs, who did not always get along.

No matter where they were in the world during this time, Jews were looked down on and life was not always good. In Russia my ancestors had not been treated well, but my parents were too young to understand this or how it had affected our people. When my parents left Russia in 1933, it was the start of a dark period in history. Adolf Hitler came to power as chancellor of Germany that January, and he immediately started discriminating against the Jews. They were defined as "inferior" and were forced out of government and university jobs. In April 1933, the Nuremberg Laws proclaimed Jews as second-class citizens. The imprisonment of Jews in concentration camps started, and many fled to what they hoped was freedom in places such as Palestine and the United States.

Even in Palestine, the Nazi attitude against Jews began to wash over the land. Arabs resented the recent influx of Jews into their country, and in October there were riots in Jerusalem, Jaffa, Haifa, and Nablus to protest the increasing numbers of Jews. It was against this backdrop that my grandparents arrived in Palestine. It was neither an easy decision nor an easy journey for them, and I can only admire those like them who did it anyway and built new lives in a new place while the world around them was becoming less and less tolerant of their existence. Ironically, during World War II, the part of Russia that my grandparents and parents came from became a sanctuary for Jews who were fleeing from their suffering elsewhere.

My family were Sephardic Jews, a part of the diaspora that

had settled in Spain and Portugal. The name comes from the Hebrew word *Sefarad*, which means *Spain*. Many Sephardic Jews were expelled from Spain as a result of the Alhambra Decree of 1492, and they spread out across Europe and North Africa and into Russia and other places. Others were killed in mass exterminations or forced to convert to Catholicism. Sephardic Jews are different from Ashkenazi Jews, who were mainly from Germany and France. However, those who campaigned against Jews and who worked to eliminate them from the world were not interested in the ethnic definitions, only in the fact that a Jew was a Jew.

As Sephardic Jews who had fled from Russia prior to World War II, my family was fortunate not to have been part of the Holocaust. However, every neighborhood in Israel was filled with Holocaust survivors and those whose families had been killed and persecuted in the atrocities. Holocaust survivors were everywhere; they were our teachers and neighbors, the families of my friends, the owners of the mini-market and the bakery, and so on. I was very curious about their experiences, so I asked them lots of questions and they told me many harrowing stories about life under Nazi rule during the war. They told me about watching their parents and brothers being killed and the terror of being rounded up and taken to concentration camps. But they also expressed that they always had hope for the future and believed that life would be better for my generation and the generations to come.

Perhaps because my own family hadn't directly experienced

the horrors of the Holocaust, I didn't realize as a child that it was such a pivotal period in history. Back then, I thought this was just what happened to people—and that it was normal.

* * *

My mother was just sixteen years old when she married my father in 1941. He was nineteen. They got married seven years before Israel would become a state, so the area was still considered Palestine back then. It was also the middle of World War II. There were several occasions between 1940 and 1942 when Axis forces controlled by Germany threatened to enter Palestine, but the British and other Allied forces kept them out. Palestine never became a battlefront and, in a rare example of cooperation, Palestinian Jews and Arabs fought side by side as part of the Allied forces to keep Germany and the Axis powers out of Palestine.

It's strange to imagine what life must have been like during that time, especially when I think of my oldest brother, Jacob. He was born in 1944, during the war. On his birth certificate, his place of birth says "Palestine." We were born in the same place, but mine says "Israel."

I was the seventh of Sara and Hanan's eight children. At first, my parents had a child every other year, starting with Jacob—who is fifteen years older than me—followed by my sister Sephora, my brother Abe, and my sister Malca. Things got off the two-year time line after that, with my sister Deborah following a year later; another sister, Mijil, seven years after that;

then me the next year; and finally my younger brother, Aetan, five years later. There's a twenty-year age difference between my oldest and youngest siblings.

The neighborhood of Tel Aviv where we grew up in is known as Shapira. It was part of central Tel Aviv, located right next to the main market and central bus station, and it's where my mother operated her restaurant with my brother Jacob's illegal casino in the back. To give an indication of how new this area was, Tel Aviv was founded in 1909 among the sand dunes north of the ancient port city of Jaffa. Shapira is even newer. It was founded by American-Jewish businessman Meir Getzl Shapiro, who moved to Palestine in 1922, about a decade before my parents arrived in Jerusalem.

If you look at maps of Palestine prior to 1910, Tel Aviv was virtually nonexistent. That changed very quickly. The Tel Aviv I grew up in was a thriving, bustling metropolis overflowing with opportunities. It embodied the hopes and dreams of Jews around the world. When I was born in 1959, Tel Aviv was by far the largest metropolitan area in Israel. Its population of seven hundred thousand was more than twice that of the next largest metropolitan area, Haifa—yet just half a century earlier, there was nothing there except sand dunes. Today it's still the largest metropolitan area in Israel, with a population of four million.

The Shapira neighborhood where I grew up is very close to the fabulous sandy beaches of the Mediterranean coast. It was like living in the Caribbean. The beaches, which stretch for miles, are among the best in the world, and I spent many memorable days hanging out there and soaking up the beautiful Mediterranean sun. The beaches were a little over a mile from my home, so I could easily walk there—and I often did, especially after school and on the weekends. It didn't matter what season it was, because the weather was always pleasant. It never got unbearably hot or uncomfortably cold, sort of like Los Angeles but more humid.

It's also interesting to me that Israel wasn't a fully formed country when I was born. The first of Israel's Basic Laws—the equivalent of the Constitution in the United States—was not established until 1958. It set forth the functions of the Knesset, the nation's parliament, and at the time of my birth, it was still the only Basic Law that had been adopted; twelve more Basic Laws were created in the years to come, fulfilling the promise of the Israeli Declaration of Independence in 1948.

The first Holocaust Memorial Day was observed on May 5, 1959, less than three months before my birth. David Ben-Gurion was the prime minister of Israel, and he won reelection later in 1959. Then, as now, not everyone was thrilled to see Israel exist as an independent nation. Our neighbors (Egypt, Jordan, Syria, and Lebanon) were actively engaged in operations against Israel, and the possibility of war was always in the air.

* * *

Israel is a very small country. A lot of people don't realize this, but the modern State of Israel is about the size of New Jersey, and the entire country would fit into the Los Angeles metropolitan area—four times over! From Tel Aviv, we could drive to any spot in Israel in only a few hours.

Even though it's so small, we didn't travel outside Israel's borders. I didn't leave the country until I was nearly fourteen, when I came to the US. I never saw a reason to leave. It was where my family was, we had the Mediterranean beaches, and we didn't have to travel far to find other beautiful scenery. Plus, of course, Israel is the Holy Land, the setting for so many events of the Jewish, Christian, and Muslim faiths. Everywhere you turn, there is a historic site, a familiar place from the Torah or the Christian Bible or the Koran. We took it for granted that we lived in the middle of such beauty and history.

Our parents took us to Jerusalem, the capital of Israel, for the first time after the Six-Day War in 1967. Jerusalem is on the border between Israel and Jordan, and during my early life, before the Six-Day War, East Jerusalem and the West Bank were controlled by Jordan. Even though Jerusalem was the capital of Israel, many of the city's most holy sites, including the old walled city that contains two of Judaism's most sacred locations, the Temple Mount and the Western Wall (also known as the Wailing Wall), were in East Jerusalem and were inaccessible to us. Because of this, there was no point in my family, or anyone else, going to Jerusalem to see the sights, despite the Torah's instruction that Jews should make three pilgrimages to Jerusalem each year: in the spring for Passover, in the summer for Shavuot, and in the fall for Sukkot.

In the Six-Day War from June 5 to 10, 1967, Jordan

attempted to take control of West Jerusalem. Israel not only repelled the attack but captured the West Bank and East Jerusalem. Israel also reunified Jerusalem, so once again it became a place where Jews could visit and fulfill their pilgrimages. In the years after the war, we'd take the train there when we could, which was two or three times a year.

We would also go to the Sea of Galilee—called Kinneret in Hebrew—which was about an hour-and-a-half drive north of Tel Aviv. Like Jerusalem, we'd go there two or three times a year. It's a beautiful spot with great beaches, and it is also the world's lowest freshwater lake at about seven hundred feet below sea level. However, its main claim to fame is that many of the stories of Jesus in the New Testament took place on its shores. It was here that Jesus delivered the Sermon on the Mount, which contains teachings such as the Beatitudes and the Lord's Prayer; where he recruited some of the apostles, including Saint Peter; and where he performed miracles such as feeding the multitude. In more recent history, it was where the first Jewish *kibbutz* (communal settlement), known as Deganya, was founded in 1909.

The other place we visited was the resort town of Eilat, which is at the very southern tip of Israel, on the Gulf of Eilat at the northern end of the Red Sea. It was about a four-hour drive from Tel Aviv. The water there was beautiful, but I didn't realize as a child that Jordan was only about a mile to the east and Egypt was about five miles to the west. These two countries were Israel's greatest detractors and enemies, and Saudi Arabia was just a few miles farther to the south.

* * *

One of the realities of growing up in Israel was the constant threat of war. Israel was a young country surrounded by Arab nations that were trying to eliminate it. Before I was born, there was the Arab–Israeli War in 1948, the years-long Palestinian Fedayeen insurgency that ended around 1956, and the Suez Crisis in 1956. After the Suez Crisis there was not a major war in Israel until the Six-Day War of 1967. I was too young at that time to realize it, but my parents and older siblings were very much aware of the threat that war could break out at any time. Just like the Holocaust tales that, to me, were just another part of life, the threat of war was also something I didn't understand but accepted as normal. Even though I was mature for my age, I rarely watched the news, so I had no idea that people in other countries were not like us and never had to worry about neighboring countries trying to eliminate them.

The only war that affected me personally was the Six-Day War, which started a few weeks before my eighth birthday in 1967. My oldest brother, Jacob, was in the Israeli Army, and he was sent off to fight in the war. Most of the action took place to the east and north of Tel Aviv near the borders with Lebanon, Syria, and Jordan, but there was some shelling of the Tel Aviv suburbs early in the war. It was only much later that the Israeli government built bunkers for the civilian population to escape to during the war. In 1967, we had a vacant property across the street from our house that had a huge trench dug in it. When the sirens went off to warn of a possible rocket attack, the whole neighborhood ran into the trench for safety. I remember waiting there with my mother and my siblings until the all-clear was given.

I don't recall having a fear of war, most likely because I didn't know what was going on or what the consequences might have been. I thought we were always at war or on the brink of war, so I didn't understand how or why this war in 1967 was different. All I knew was that there were now new rules and, as a kid, I just accepted those rules. For example, we couldn't turn the lights on in our homes at night, and car headlights were painted blue so they wouldn't shine and become targets.

As a kid, I also didn't know that the war involved all of Israel as well as the surrounding countries. I had no sense of what was going on beyond my neighborhood, so I thought the war was happening only in Shapira or only in the few blocks around our house. I can't say I noticed any hardships other than the blackouts and having to hide in the trench, and thankfully no bombs or rockets came close to hitting us. The war was over quickly, and life returned to normal in no time.

Israel's next war was the War of Attrition on the Sinai Peninsula from 1967 to 1970, followed by the Yom Kippur War in 1973. Tel Aviv was far away from the War of Attrition, and by 1973 I was already safe in Los Angeles, half a world away.

* * *

I am fortunate to come from a line of industrious people. My grandparents spoke Russian and Uzbek, but they spoke to their children and grandchildren in Hebrew. My mother's father didn't go to school, but he was able to support his wife and family in Jerusalem. Before my parents married, they were willing to do anything and accept any job in Jerusalem in order to make money. My mother started off as a maid, cleaning homes for wealthy people, and my father built roads. He wasn't allowed to serve in the Israeli Army because of a minor disability. Israel was just getting started as a new nation and needed every soldier to contribute and to defend the nation; it was a huge disappointment for me to learn later in life that my father had not been in the Israeli Army.

The first thing my parents did when they got married was to move to Tel Aviv. It was where they wanted to begin their new life together and where they wanted to raise a family and contribute to Israel's future. My grandparents followed them to Tel Aviv, and a few years later my grandfather opened a mini-market in the city—and my father followed his example by opening a mini-market of his own.

My mother was a go-getter with unlimited energy, but my father was more laid-back. I was more like my mother, and I always had a plan to make a little money. When I was about nine or ten, I started raising pigeons that I kept in rows of cages on the roof of our house. They were homing pigeons, so I would release them from the roof and watch them fly away and then come back home, which they always did because they knew I was providing them with food and shelter. I had a great love for those birds, and I think they understood that and loved me back.

There were all kinds of pigeons in those cages, and some of them were really beautiful and expensive. I would buy them for three or four lirot, which was the currency in Israel when I was a kid, and after I raised them and trained them to fly home, I sold them for five or six lirot. It was a great lesson in creating a successful business model, working hard, and making a profit.

I bought and sold pigeons right up until the point when I came to America at the age of almost fourteen. While I was running my pigeon business, I was also buying and selling bicycles and cards that were like baseball cards but instead had pictures of movie stars and famous soccer players on them. In addition, I always had a pocketful of change from the tips I received from working at my mother's restaurant. Even as a young kid, I was a go-getter who was wheeling and dealing all day long. It was the perfect preparation for my life in Los Angeles, where the skills I'd learned as a boy set me up to live the life I'd always dreamed about.

CHAPTER 3

ABE

I have always had a huge connection to all my siblings, but growing up, my brother Abe in particular was my absolute hero and the coolest guy around. We've always been close, and we still get together every Friday at my house. Whenever anyone asks why there's such a tight bond between us, I tell them a story that happened a few years before I came to America, back in the early 1970s. I was eleven years old, and Abe was twice my age at that time. He had a new girlfriend—the one he ended up marrying—and lots of "groovy" sophisticated friends.

I didn't see Abe every day, because he lived in his own place. One day I was hanging out with some friends a couple of blocks from our house when Abe drove by. His car was full of his friends and he was towing a small boat. Stopping the car, Abe called me over and asked me what I was doing. "Just hanging out with friends," I told him. "Where are you going with the boat?"

He told me that he and his friends were on the way to the Sea of Galilee for a few days. "Do you want to join us?" he asked.

Here was my brother, about twenty-two years old, with a car filled with his friends and their girlfriends, and I'm sure the last thing they wanted for their weekend away was Abe's kid brother tagging along.

"Abe, don't do that," his friends complained. "Why do you want to bring him with us? He's a young kid. He'll be in the way."

"Look, guys," Abe told them, "he's my priority. You're in my car, and my brother is coming with us. Anyone who doesn't like it, go get a taxi."

Abe told me to run home and pack some clothes, and he'd wait for me. A few minutes later, I was on the road to the Sea of Galilee, squeezed into the back seat of the car with Abe's friends, having fun and listening to music.

I have never forgotten my brother's words that day: "He's my priority." Those words sum up what a great guy Abe was and how he'd do anything for his family—even risk losing friends. Fortunately, his friends tolerated me for the next few days, even though I was only eleven. Abe didn't lose any friends, and nobody had to get a taxi.

Another time, when I was about thirteen, I was walking the streets of Tel Aviv with my cousin Yoni when we saw two pretty girls smoking on a balcony. They were a little older than us, and I recognized one of them as a friend of Abe's, so we went up to them and asked if we could have a cigarette. They looked at us and the girl who was Abe's friend said, "Aren't you a bit young to smoke? Are you sure you want one?" I didn't really smoke, but it seemed cool and the girls were cute, so I said, "Sure!" We hung out a little and smoked on their balcony with them.

The next day when I ran into Abe, he opened up a pack of cigarettes, shoved it in front of my face, and said, "Here. Take one." I hesitated, because I didn't want him to know I'd started smoking.

"I don't smoke," I told him.

"But I heard you're a smoker now. Take one and smoke with me."

"Please don't do this to me," I said.

"So now you're lying to me?" he asked, and he hit me with the back of his hand. It startled me, and it stung. He was my brother, which made it hurt even more. "So you didn't smoke last night?" The girls must have told him about the previous night.

"It was nothing," I said, hoping he'd believe my lie. "I was just kidding around."

That incident taught me a lot, but mainly it taught me not to lie to my brother or to anyone else because they'd find out the truth. Abe was the most loving and considerate guy, but he was also tough and a disciplinarian when he needed to be, like a second father. I never smoked again in my life . . . except for the occasional cigar.

When I moved to Los Angeles the next year, Abe was already living there, and when I opened my burger joints, he always encouraged me and sometimes even lent a hand. He helped me clean, paint the walls, and get everything in order, and he was very tech-savvy. If I needed a loan to get my businesses up and running, I knew I could count on him for that too. He was always there for me, and I tried to be there for him.

*   *   *

Abe was a champion wrestler and, if not for a decision that baffled me at the time, his talent probably would have led to his untimely death in a deadly terrorist attack that shocked the world in 1972.

Abe was a highly trained Greco-Roman wrestler. In my mind, this was the purest form of wrestling because it relies on power and tactics. Greco-Roman wrestlers are forbidden from holding below the waist, so it takes a lot of strength to throw an opponent and to keep him down. As a result, my brother had tremendous upper body strength, and even though he was a lightweight fighter and was only about five feet eight, nobody messed with him. He had no fear of taking on much larger and heavier opponents, whether it was in the ring or in real life.

Many of Abe's wrestling matches were in Maccabi, in northern Tel Aviv, and I'd go to them whenever I could. I'm sure I had the biggest grin in the entire arena when my brother appeared. He was a delight to watch in action, and at least in my memory, he always won.

Abe was so good and was such a phenomenal talent that he easily qualified for the Israeli team for the 1972 Olympic Games in Munich, which was to be held in West Germany. For most athletes, win or lose, going to the Olympics is the pinnacle of their career, especially for someone from a small, new nation such as Israel that had limited experience at the Olympics. Just being an Olympic athlete was an honor that would set my brother apart from others and would ensure his place in Israeli history.

Israel first competed in the Olympic Games in 1952, and when Abe qualified in 1972, fewer than one hundred Israeli athletes had ever been to the Olympics. No wrestlers had ever been good enough to represent Israel, and no athletes in any sport had ever won a medal. Unlike nations such as the US, France, or Great Britain, Israel did not have a deep sporting tradition. Nevertheless, I was bursting with pride for Abe. I knew he would come home not only with Israel's *first* Olympic medal but also with a brilliant *gold* medal. He would become a hero in Israel. My brother, my role model, the greatest wrestler in the entire world!

But things didn't quite work out that way. I was thirteen as the Olympics approached in late August. Abe was twenty-four, and he already had a wife, a good job, a car, and a nice home in Tel Aviv. The Olympic Games at this time was amateur level, meaning there was no financial incentive to take part. Abe still had to pay his mortgage, so it created a conflict. Regardless of the prestige of being an Olympian, he was likely to lose money and maybe miss a mortgage payment if he focused all his energy on training. To encourage people like Abe to stay in Israel and to raise their families there, the Israeli government offered interest-free loans to buy homes. My mother, who owned a profitable restaurant with my brother Jacob, had assisted Abe in getting a loan and helped him with a substantial down payment so his monthly note would be affordable.

The period to pay back the loan was very short, only about twenty-four to thirty-six months, so it was essential to have a job to enable you to make the payments. Abe had that job, and he was close to paying off the loan. He was making good money at a business that was something like an early Amazon, which promised next-day delivery. It was a revolutionary idea, and it was thriving in Tel Aviv, where the hustle and bustle rivaled that of any large city in the world.

Unfortunately, my mother didn't understand the importance of the Olympic Games. To her it was just another competition, except this time it meant Abe would have to leave his job for several weeks during the summer when business was usually strong. She was afraid his job wouldn't be there when he got back and that maybe he would miss a payment on his loan. I don't know the exact argument she used, but she convinced him not to go to Munich. I don't think Abe recognized at the time how important going to the Olympics was, not just to himself and his family but to Israel.

I was just a kid, so I didn't understand the pressures of having a job and a family. All I knew was that something wasn't right when someone like Abe couldn't go to the most important competition of his life at the greatest sporting spectacle the world had ever known. Three other wrestlers became the first to represent Israel at the Olympics.

I was heartbroken when I watched the opening ceremony of the 1972 Olympic Games in Munich on August 26. I knew my big brother should have been part of the Israeli team that marched into Olympic Stadium to join the thousands of others who represented the fastest, strongest, and best athletes in the world. I envisioned him being the flag bearer for his country, making an incredible statement about Israel and the Jewish people returning to Germany a generation after the horror of the Holocaust, but I knew he was at home in Tel Aviv, perhaps pondering this missed opportunity.

* * *

Ten days later, on September 5, 1972, the world changed. Early in the morning, while the Israeli Olympic team and their coaches were sleeping in the Olympic Village, eight Palestine Liberation Organization (PLO) terrorists from the militant Black September faction bypassed security and entered the Olympic Village. They scaled a chain-link fence, and even though they were seen by other athletes, they were mistaken for Olympians because they wore tracksuits and carried duffel bags. They looked like regular athletes sneaking back into the Olympic Village after a night out, except that their duffel bags held AKM (Kalashnikov) assault rifles, Tokarev pistols, and hand grenades.

The PLO was essentially an enemy of Israel. It was committed to the extinction of Israel as a nation and establishing Arab control over the land. The group was founded in 1964, and it began its terrorist attacks on Israel the following year. By 1972, its attacks were becoming more frequent, and the group had become known for hijacking passenger airplanes, particularly those associated with Israel. The Black September faction even assassinated the Jordanian prime minister in late 1971.

The terrorists knew exactly which apartments housed the Israeli delegation. As the masked men started to break into the first apartment, where Israeli coaches and officials were staying, wrestling referee Yossef Gutfreund attempted in vain to stop them. Although weightlifting coach Tuvia Sokolovsky managed to escape through a window, the others staying there were taken hostage. In another apartment, the terrorists took Israel's three wrestlers and three weightlifters as additional hostages.

When the guerrilla attack started, the Israelis tried to fight back, but the terrorists were ruthless and had firearms. Weightlifter Yossef Romano and wrestling coach Moshe Weinberg were shot and killed in the struggle, but freestyle wrestler Gad Tsobari was fortunate to escape. Meanwhile, Holocaust survivor and racewalker Shaul Ladany, who had been imprisoned at the Bergen-Belsen concentration camp in Germany as a child during World War II, was awoken by the commotion and jumped to safety from the balcony of his neighboring apartment. He was the first to raise the alarm.

Nine hostages remained, including freestyle wrestler Eliezer Halfin and Greco-Roman wrestler Mark Slavin. All were tightly bound and severely beaten as the day progressed and the terrible news spread around the world. Millions of people watched anxiously as the standoff continued. Israeli prime minister Golda Meir and US president Richard Nixon joined a chorus of condemnation of the shocking terrorist tactics, especially at a worldwide event devoted to peace and brotherhood.

In exchange for the nine hostages, the PLO demanded the release of 234 Palestinians and other prisoners held by Israel. It was Israel's policy not to negotiate with terrorists, so the Israeli government refused the offer. Nonetheless, the West German authorities agreed to provide two helicopters and a Boeing 727 jet so the terrorists could escape to Cairo, Egypt. Late at night, escaping under the cover of darkness and taking the hostages as collateral, the terrorists attempted to flee.

Suddenly and without warning at a little past midnight on September 6, the whole situation turned into a bloodbath. The terrorists feared they were being ambushed, so they massacred all nine hostages. Five of the eight terrorists were also killed.

Legendary US sports announcer Jim McKay of ABC broke the news solemnly to American viewers: "Our worst fears have been realized tonight. . . . They're all gone."

The Olympic Games were suspended for a day, and a memorial was held for the slain Israelis on September 6 at Olympic Stadium in Munich. After the service, the remaining Israeli team left Munich and returned in shock and mourning to Israel. Later, memorial plaques were placed in Munich Olympic Park and in front of the apartments in the Olympic Village where the hostages had been taken. In response to the attack and massacre, Prime Minister Meir authorized Operation Wrath of God to track down and kill the three surviving terrorists, who unbelievably were released by West Germany a few weeks later in a hostage exchange for a hijacked German Lufthansa airplane. Since then, two of the terrorists were allegedly killed by Mossad, the Israeli national intelligence agency.

*   *   *

The devastating series of events in Munich were over in less than twenty-four hours, but it seemed like everything happened in slow motion and went on for days. From the moment the news broke, it was the only topic on the television and radio in Tel Aviv. It happened on a weekday, so I had to go to school. But nobody could concentrate on anything else. I recall listening to the radio at school for updates, and when I got home, the black-and-white TV was on with the reassuring voice of Haim Yavin telling us all the latest details, right through to the awful massacre.

It didn't escape notice that if not for a decision I couldn't comprehend at the time, my brother Abe would have been one of the hostages and most likely would have been massacred. He would have been in the apartment with the wrestlers and weightlifters when the terrorists broke in and attacked.

What made everything even more tense and tragic is that we knew the wrestlers who were killed, Eliezer Halfin and Mark Slavin, and Gad Tsobari, who escaped, as well as the weight-lifters. Yossef Romano, who was the second person to be killed when he tried to stop the terrorists from coming in, was my brother's best friend, and weightlifter David Berger used to hang out at the beach with us. Yossef was four years older than Abe, so he was like an older brother to him. He was often over at our house, joking around and sharing a meal with us.

The first two were killed early in the day, but the news never mentioned their names. I don't think anybody knew who had been killed; they just said that one person was dead. Then two people were dead. We didn't know at the time that they were Yossef Romano and Moshe Weinberg.

Watching and waiting as the events unfolded in Munich was agony, but for Abe it was also personal, and he felt every ounce of pain and fear that his friends were going through. He would have swapped places with them if he could. We watched in stunned silence, but until the massacre happened, Abe was exceptionally positive that they'd all get out alive and would be home in a day or two. He couldn't wait for them to come home, and he was already planning to treat them to the biggest dinner and the biggest party of their lives. Just a few hours later, they were all dead.

When it was all over, Abe felt guilty about not being there and not being able to do something to save his friends and fellow Israelis. "I probably could have made a difference," he told us. "Maybe I could have stopped the terrorists from going in." As much as I loved and worshiped my brother, though, I don't think even he could have done anything when up against a bunch of terrorists with assault rifles who had no respect for human life.

DREAMS DON'T DIE

The massacre in Munich was devastating. It's still something we talk about today, and it shows that we can't take anything for granted because we don't know what tomorrow will bring. For me, the most mind-boggling thing about the whole situation was that what I believed at the time to be Abe's stupidity in not going to Munich actually saved his life. It was also a huge wake-up call that contributed to my family moving from Israel to the United States in the coming years.

CHAPTER 4
THE CASINO

From the time I was about ten, my mother and oldest brother, Jacob, owned a restaurant and bar in Tel Aviv. It was just four blocks from our house, so my mother walked to work there every day. Dozens of neighborhood restaurants and bars just like it were scattered across the city, but this one was different. It had an illegal casino in the back.

Jacob ran the casino, which was nothing more than a space with no air conditioning and no windows. It had six card tables in the main room and two card tables in a side room for high rollers, but it didn't have roulette wheels, slot machines, or any of the trappings usually associated with modern casinos. A few ceiling fans didn't do much except circulate the smoke-filled air. As a result, the place always smelled of cigarettes and stale beer. Some of the regulars were not the nicest people you'd ever meet, but that's where I wanted to be, right in the middle of the action. In reality, it wasn't much more than a clubhouse where the locals could gamble on poker, but to me, it was Monte Carlo.

The restaurant and casino were located on a fairly busy commercial side street, with a couple of tables set outside where people could sit in peace to enjoy a coffee and read the newspaper. The food was pretty standard—sandwiches, pastries, and other menu items that were easy to make—and, of course, there was a lot of coffee being sold, because Israelis drink more coffee than almost anyone else in the world.

Businesses like this in Israel were set up in a similar way to what is happening in many American cities now, with a retail business on the ground floor and residential areas above. Today we call it mixed use, but back then in Israel, it was just the standard setup. I'm not sure if there was any zoning or if this type of arrangement even had a name.

Across the street from the restaurant was a motorcycle shop, and within half a block were a bank, a synagogue, a mini-market, another restaurant, and a fruit and vegetable shop, each with apartments above, so you were never far from everything you needed. It was the type of commercial and residential street that was typical of almost any neighborhood in Tel Aviv.

The restaurant was a good business that made money, and we lived well. Unlike a proper casino in Monte Carlo or Las Vegas, though, there was no "house money," nor were there any card dealers in the casino, so Jacob never got a cut of the winnings. It was more like a series of poker games being held in someone's garage or living room. Sometimes there were disagreements and fights, but generally everyone got along because they were there to have fun. Jacob made money by renting tables to the poker players and controlling the chips. The guys who gambled also drank a lot of whiskey and beer and smoked a lot of cigarettes, and the longer they stayed and the more they drank and smoked, the more money he made.

By the time I was twelve, I was spending more and more time at the restaurant after school and on weekends, helping out where I could. That's also about the time when people started calling me "Ringo" because I'd grown my hair long and they thought it made me look like Ringo Starr of the Beatles. I took it as a compliment, and I had dreams of one day being as rich and famous as Ringo.

At first, I did odd jobs like clearing tables and bringing people their food and drinks, but I also learned how to make Turkish coffee, which was very popular in Israel. There is a fine art to making Turkish coffee, but the basic ingredient is finely ground coffee beans that are cooked with water in a small, long-handled copper pot called a *finjan*. I paid attention to the way people wanted their coffee, and they loved the way I made it.

I also brought huge quantities of whiskey and beer to the guys playing poker in the back, which is where I'd make the most money from tips. I would pick up just a few coins here and there, but it added up quickly, especially when I combined it with the money I'd already made from selling pigeons and trading bicycles. It was easy money, and it gave me a sense of freedom that most kids my age didn't have.

I didn't realize it at the time, but every day working at the restaurant and in the casino was a learning experience for me. I learned how the business ran, from figuring out the workings of the kitchen and the bar to managing the staff and ordering supplies. I also learned how to read people, especially if they were up to no good. It didn't seem all that difficult or complicated to me, and when I opened my own burger joints in Los Angeles a few years later, all this knowledge fell into place and made it so much easier to get my businesses up and running.

* * *

Gambling of any kind has always been illegal in Israel, but Israelis love to play cards and gamble anyway. It didn't take long for word to get around that there was a casino in the back of the restaurant, and there was always a steady stream of customers. It was a full-time business for Jacob, but it was separated from the restaurant by a heavy-duty metal door that was not easy to open. Most of the casino customers came through the back door, which led to an alley.

Not surprisingly, the casino was also known to the police, who made frequent raids in an attempt to shut it down. The police confiscated the cards and casino chips, hoping to make it impossible to keep the casino open. Those things were very expensive, especially the casino chips, because they were black-market items that Jacob had to order from some shady characters. My brother usually ended up in court after a raid and was given huge fines. He'd always pay the fines, then go right out and buy brand-new cards and chips so he could open the casino again.

The raids usually started with undercover officers who were playing cards in the casino. The officers' mistakes were starting the raids in the restaurant, which gave everyone in the casino enough time to try to get rid of the cards and chips before the police came through the metal door. There was also a bell in the casino that warned of a raid, and by the time the police managed to open the door, most of the players had escaped through the back door. Eventually, the police got smarter and ambushed the back door as well to stop the players from getting away.

At the start of one raid, my sister-in-law (Jacob's wife) gathered all the cards and chips and crammed them into a bag. I was only twelve, but she handed me the bag and told me to walk out of the casino with it and take it home. She thought the police would never suspect a twelve-year-old kid of being part of the casino operation. I knew precisely what was going on, but I acted cool. One of the undercover officers in civilian clothes stopped me anyway and grabbed the bag. He asked me what was in it and what I was doing with it, and I told him I'd just picked it up and didn't know what was in it. I was only twelve, so nothing happened to me, but the police got the cards and the chips.

When you live in that kind of environment, you're not scared of the police or of what may happen when they come busting in. It's just a part of life. I'm not even sure the police were really trying to shut down the casino, because it was connected to my mother's restaurant, which was a legitimate business. They never touched the restaurant, only the casino, but they came back every few weeks.

* * *

One of the locals who often came into the casino was Tommy Goldberg. He'd watched too many American gangster movies and thought he was a wiseguy. Plus, he nursed a nasty drug habit, which made him a bit of a wild card. Still, he was a regular customer who spent a lot of time and money in the casino, so Jacob tolerated him. But Tommy didn't like to lose and had a cruel sense of humor—a combination that almost proved deadly.

The busboy and dishwasher at the restaurant was a guy named Frishka. He was in his forties and was a little slow mentally. Everyone liked him and he did his job well, but for someone like Tommy, Frishka was an easy target for a cheap laugh. Tommy had been playing cards with his gang in the casino for a while one evening, and he was making fun of Frishka in his usual belittling style. He decided to bet one of the guys in his gang that Frishka couldn't tell the difference between beer and urine, and to make his point, he urinated into a half-empty bottle of beer and invited Frishka over to their table. He challenged Frishka to chug the "beer" to see who could finish it the fastest.

Someone at the next table overheard the plan and alerted my sister-in-law, who was tending bar that night. She couldn't find Jacob, so she called me over and told me what Tommy and his gang were about to do. I ran straight into the back room, and just as Frishka was about to start chugging the sickening mixture of beer and urine, I knocked the bottle away from his mouth, spilling it all over the table and onto Tommy and his gangsters. They were so taken by surprise that two or three of them fell backward in their chairs as they tried to avoid the airborne arc of urine and beer.

I was just thirteen at the time, but I had no fear of standing up to Tommy and his gang of thugs. I have never been a fearful guy—then or now. I stood up to him because my gut told me to and because I knew Tommy was trying to humiliate a guy who was just trying to do his job.

Tommy was not exactly thrilled that I'd spoiled his fun and gotten urine over his cards and his friends. When I looked into his drug-addled red eyes, I saw pure rage directed at me, and when he charged toward me, I braced for what I knew was coming. Just then, Jacob burst in and ordered Tommy to back off. Luckily for me, he stopped—but he was still steaming mad, and his gang was itching for a fight. To defuse the tense atmosphere, Jacob sent me home. But things got much worse a few weeks later.

Tommy still held a grudge against Jacob and especially against me, and he had been banned from the restaurant and casino. One night, though, he and his gang came looking for trouble and became belligerent when they were asked to leave. They got into a huge argument with Jacob, which led to punches being thrown. Jacob was outnumbered and was getting pretty well beaten, but my brother Abe—the champion wrestler—was in the next room and came barreling through the door to his rescue. Within a few seconds, my brothers had beaten Tommy's gang and they were lying on the floor.

That's when Tommy pulled out a handgun and shot Abe in the head at point-blank range.

* * *

News of the fight traveled back to me quickly, and I rushed to the hospital. Incredibly, Abe had been wounded but not killed. The bullet only grazed his forehead, and he's still got the scar to this day. If Tommy's aim had been even an inch to the right, it would have killed Abe instantly. To me, it was a miracle that Abe wasn't seriously injured or killed, just like it was a miracle that his decision not to go to the Munich Olympics in 1972 most likely saved his life. He'd escaped death twice in only a few months.

I waited in Abe's room, watching him lying there with a bloody bandage wrapped around his head and knowing that he'd literally come within an inch of losing his life. I felt as if it were my fault that he'd been shot and that Jacob had been beaten up. It was so confusing; I knew I'd done the right thing in protecting Frishka. But doing the right thing had led to my brothers getting into a gunfight with gangsters.

When Abe finally woke up, I broke down and told him how sorry I was for getting him shot. He wasn't upset, and he never blamed me. "You did the right thing," he told me. "Sometimes doing the right thing lands you in a pile of trouble. Most of the time, you come out smelling like a rose. What matters is doing what you think is right." It was so reassuring to hear those words.

Little by little, things went back to normal, but they were never quite the same. Tommy was taken off to jail, but we were worried about his gang and what they might do to get revenge. The police also shut the whole place—restaurant and casino—down while they investigated the shooting. That was the final straw. My mother decided not to reopen the restaurant, and my brother closed the casino for good.

The pressure of everything—Tommy and his gangsters, Abe getting shot in the head, the trauma of the Munich Olympics, the restaurant closing, and the ever-present threat of war—became too much for our family. Tel Aviv didn't feel safe anymore, and soon Jacob and Abe left Israel to seek a new life in the United States. Their plan was to put roots down there, become established, and then send word to the rest of the family to join them.

Meanwhile, I went back to the beach whenever I had the chance. A few weeks later, I was there with my cousin Yoni when I was attacked without warning by three older kids in the restroom. I was on the floor before I'd even had a chance to fight back, and I went home with a black eye, a bloodied face, and several sore ribs. I'd never seen the kids before, and they didn't say anything to me, but I assumed they were with Tommy's people and they'd beaten me up as payback for Tommy ending up in jail.

* * *

Without the restaurant and casino, I didn't know what to do with my time during summer vacation in 1973, so I found a job with a bookstore, delivering books on my bike. It was a great way to make up for some of the money I was missing from getting tips in the casino. Plus, every day my mother would make me a wonderful lunch to take with me. Working for the bookstore was quite different from working in the restaurant and casino. I didn't have to deal with customers or put up with fights and arguments, and I got to ride around on my bike all day long. It seemed a perfect job, even if it wasn't all that challenging most of the time.

One day before lunch, a couple of months before my fourteenth birthday, I was given a book to deliver to someone in northern Tel Aviv. I'd been up there before, and I figured it was only about a ten-minute ride away from the bookstore, so it would be a quick job and I'd get back to enjoy my lunch before setting off again with the next book. But it was a terrible day with a heavy rain, and it turned out that I didn't know the neighborhood as well as I'd thought.

Today it would be simple to find an unfamiliar location with GPS and mapping apps, but in 1973, I had to figure it out on my own without a map, and it was even more difficult to tell where I was going because of the constant rain. I got lost many times, but I was determined to deliver the book. I was trying to act like a man, so I never turned around. Instead, when I got close to where I thought the address was, I asked several people for directions. Nobody knew for sure, or they thought they knew but actually ended up sending me in the wrong direction.

It would have been easy to give up and go back to the

bookstore and tell them it was raining too hard or I couldn't find the address—but that's not the way I am. In the end, I found the address and delivered the book. Once I committed to delivering it, I made sure it was delivered, even in the torrential rain and even though it took me all afternoon to find the address.

When I finally got back to the bookstore, it was about 5:00 p.m. and too late for the next delivery. Only then was I able to eat my lunch. I often think about that day in the rain, riding my bike all over northern Tel Aviv but never giving up. I was not going to be defeated by something as simple as an address. Working in the casino had taught me how important it is to care for others, and now, working in the bookstore, I was learning how to always finish what I started.

CHAPTER 5

LOS ANGELES

A couple of months before I started working at the bookstore, Jacob and Abe decided to leave Tel Aviv for the United States. After all the drama with the casino and Abe being shot in the head, it turned out to be a fairly easy decision. They were both quite a bit older than me, but they still had their futures to consider and no longer felt safe in Israel. Abe was twenty-four and newly married, and his wife was pregnant with their first child. Jacob was twenty-eight and already had four children, but he and Abe decided they could no longer stay in Tel Aviv—and with the restaurant and casino closed, there was nothing other than family keeping them in Israel. Of course, the plan was that the whole family would eventually move to the US to join them.

Jacob and Abe left Israel in the spring of 1973, after the restaurant and casino closed but shortly before I was attacked in the restroom at the beach. They never knew about me getting beaten up until much later because my mother didn't want to upset them while they were trying to start their new lives halfway around the world.

In many respects, my family pulling up roots and moving—not just to the next street or the next town but to a new country and a different continent—was not unusual or unexpected. For thousands of years, Jews had been on the move, usually as migrants but sometimes as refugees. Just two generations earlier, my own grandparents had arrived in Israel from Russia, and at some point before that, their ancestors had left Western Europe and eventually ended up in Russia. History repeats itself.

Even though Israel was the Promised Land, the United States was the home of big visionaries and offered more of just about everything. It was a place where dreamers and opportunists like me could see their ideas come true and where hard work is often rewarded.

The original goal was for Jacob and Abe to settle in New York, where they had friends who had moved there from Tel Aviv. From the movies and things they'd heard over the years, they thought New York was the place to be, especially for new immigrants from Israel who they figured would easily be accepted in the city.

They arrived in New York City full of hope and excitement. The city was electrifying and the nation was brimming with possibilities. At about the same time they set foot in New York, the Vietnam War finally came to an end after years of bitter conflict that had torn the nation apart. Israel still faced the constant threat of war and annihilation from its neighbors, but America was at peace and my brothers could look forward to raising their children here without the threat of war.

Everything seemed better in the US. Even the gangsters were better. Everyone was talking about *The Godfather*, which had just won the Oscar for Best Picture, and its realistic portrayal of a Mafia kingdom. When I saw it for the first time, I couldn't help but think that this was how Tommy Goldberg and his gang saw themselves, instead of as the small-time hooligans they really were.

As they flew into New York, my brothers looked out the airplane windows and saw for the first time the Statue of Liberty in New York Harbor, which had beckoned immigrants to the promise of America for nearly a century. Just a short distance away were the newly completed Twin Towers of the World Trade Center rising above the city as a modern symbol of the American Dream. They didn't know it at the time, but this was the start of a new era of hope and prosperity in American history, and they had chosen the perfect moment to arrive and to make their own way in this new world.

It was cold and windy when Jacob and Abe arrived in New York, and the city was experiencing a late burst of winter weather. It was wetter and colder than usual, and it felt especially uncomfortable for two guys coming from sunny Tel Aviv. They struggled to stay warm—and to stay optimistic. But they couldn't get used to New York, and within a month they had made a plan to return to Tel Aviv and get their lives back in order in Israel.

By chance, an old friend of Jacob's from Tel Aviv who was living in Los Angeles convinced him to come out to California for a visit before he and Abe went back to Israel. So Jacob flew out to Los Angeles, expecting only to visit his friend for a few days, and then fly back to New York and onward to Israel with Abe. To his great surprise, he absolutely loved Los Angeles, and he called his wife and Abe from there. "Come out here to LA and bring our families," he said. "We're not going back to Israel."

*　*　*

It broke my heart to see my brothers—my role models and heroes—leave Tel Aviv. I was excited for them, but I also started wondering whether I'd ever see them again. When we got word that they'd decided to live in Los Angeles instead of New York, that seemed even farther away. I knew LA was the home of Hollywood and movie stars and sunshine, but I had no idea what else might have drawn them there.

My mother knew how much I missed my brothers, so one afternoon in July she surprised me with an airline ticket to Los Angeles. "You're flying in a few days," she told me as she handed me the ticket. "Happy birthday!" I'd never flown anywhere, and I'd never left Israel before, so I had to rush to the passport office with my mother and then hurriedly pack for my trip. I was bursting with excitement, though, and it felt like the happiest time of my life.

I left Tel Aviv a week before my fourteenth birthday.

Back in 1973, there were no direct flights from Israel to Los Angeles, so like Jacob and Abe a few months earlier, my first stop was in New York. I stayed there for a few days with family friends and saw some distant relatives. During the day, I rode the subway and walked around the city by myself, visiting the Empire State Building, the Statue of Liberty, and Times Square (which was pretty seedy back then), but most of all just soaking up the city's energy.

I'm not sure a lot of families would allow a nearly fourteen-year-old child to wander freely around New York by himself, but I was a mature and savvy kid, and I was able to entertain myself quite easily with the sights and sounds of the city. The commotion and the constant movement of the people there spoke to me, but my mind was focused on the next flight and seeing my brothers again for the first time in several months.

A few days later, I took a flight from New York to Los Angeles. When I stepped off the plane, there were my brothers. It was the greatest feeling to see them again. They were renting an apartment in Van Nuys in the San Fernando Valley, one of the fast-growing LA suburbs at that time. In Los Angeles lingo, it's where the 101 and 405 highways meet, so it's easy to get there from almost anywhere.

As we drove from the airport to my brothers' apartment, I was fascinated by the multilane highways and how many cars were on them. It was so different from the people and traffic that filled the streets of New York and the narrow, constricted roads in Tel Aviv, and already I could tell that everyone here in

LA was trying to get somewhere else in a hurry. Also, everyone was driving. I didn't see a single pedestrian. I didn't know if it was the blazing sun or the huge distances that kept people from walking, but it immediately struck me that this was a city built for cars—and as someone who'd always dreamed of owning nice cars and being able to race my cousins along wide, empty roads, I started to feel a sense of belonging right away.

My brothers' three-bedroom apartment was near the intersection of Van Nuys Boulevard and Oxnard Street, a busy place with lots of traffic, people, and businesses. For a fourteen-year-old kid from Israel, this seemed to be what Los Angeles was all about, and it was thrilling to be in the center of it all. Even better, their apartment complex was the greatest thing I'd ever seen in my life. There was a huge courtyard in the middle and a fabulous swimming pool with a diving board. You opened the door to the apartment, and there was the pool—and it was never crowded. It felt like heaven.

It blew my mind that you could actually have a swimming pool at your home. The first swimming pool I ever saw was the one the city built beside the beach in Tel Aviv in the 1960s. It was a public pool for everyone in Tel Aviv, so it was always crowded, but I hung out there a lot with my cousins and friends. Today, private swimming pools are everywhere in Israel, but they were so rare back then that I'd never seen one before. At that time, Israel was barely twenty-five years old and was somehow surviving with all the Arab countries around it trying to elimi-nate it, so swimming pools were the ultimate luxury. The idea of having a private pool was beyond my imagination, and here in LA it seemed like my brothers had made it to the big time.

A few days after I arrived, I celebrated my fourteenth birthday with my brothers and their wives and children in Los Angeles. After a month in LA, I was supposed to go back to Tel Aviv and back to school, but I was so happy here on the West Coast that I didn't want to leave, and so I stayed. Eventually, my parents flew out to Los Angeles to visit my brothers—and to pick me up and bring me back with them, but they ended up loving it and staying as well. They had already managed to sell the restaurant in Tel Aviv, so they didn't have a reason to go back to Israel right away.

Our family was slowly reuniting in Los Angeles, and what was supposed to be a monthlong visit to see my brothers looked like it was turning into a lifetime adventure.

* * *

By the time my parents arrived in Los Angeles to get me, Jacob had moved to a house in Pomona, which is about an hour east of downtown but still part of Greater Los Angeles. He had bought a beautiful and famous restaurant, Badon's, from the owner, who was retiring. Jacob knew all about operating a restaurant from his time in Tel Aviv; the only difference with Badon's was the food, which was American, but he adapted quickly and made the restaurant successful. He'd also given up on the idea of the casino, so there was no illegal activity in the back.

Meanwhile, I stayed in Van Nuys with Abe and his wife and enrolled at Van Nuys High School. In early 1974, about a year after he arrived in America, Abe moved to an apartment in Hollywood—and I moved there with him and transferred to Hollywood High School. My parents sold their house and everything else in Israel and rented a small apartment in the same complex as Abe, so I moved in with them. Not long after that, they bought a house on Crescent Heights Boulevard in the Fairfax District near Beverly Hills and Hollywood. They invested everything in America.

My parents chose the Fairfax District because a large number of European Jews had settled there after World War II. Many of the residents were Holocaust survivors. It was a neighborhood with farmers market–style grocery stores and other small businesses, so it reminded them of Israel. It was almost like having their Shapira community back. Close by were the famous La Brea Tar Pits and the CBS Television City, where CBS had its West Coast television network operations. Today, the upscale Grove and Beverly Center shopping centers are close by, but the area still has much of the same feel as it did in the 1970s. Years later, after my parents passed away, we kept the house on Crescent Heights Boulevard in the family, and we still own it to this day.

Like generations of immigrants before us, the Shomofs were becoming Americans, and little by little, we were starting to get our own piece of the American Dream.

* * *

Hollywood High was an interesting place, but I didn't stay there for long, and I wasn't really interested in school anyway. A lot of the kids at school lived in Hollywood and were the sons and daughters of movie stars and other people in the movie industry, but that lifestyle has never appealed to me. And as the freshman Israeli kid with a funny accent, I didn't fit in very well and didn't have many friends at school.

What's more, I barely spoke English when I arrived in Los Angeles, so I had to take English lessons on top of all my other classes. Today almost everyone in Israel speaks English, which is required as a second language in schools and universities and is essential for almost any type of business in the modern economy. Back in the 1970s, though, it was rare to hear people in Israel speaking English.

I wanted more than school could offer, so I started looking for ways to earn money. My mother was also trying to earn some money, so she asked the rabbi at the nearby synagogue if he knew of any jobs that were available. There were a lot of very rich Jewish people living in the neighborhood, and my mother started working as a housecleaner for some of them. It was something she knew how to do, as it was the same work she had done back when she was starting her adult life in Israel.

One summer afternoon in 1974, when I was almost fifteen, I needed to see my mother, so I rode my bike over to the house where she was working and knocked on the door. She answered, but she was horrified to see me.

"What are you doing here?" she demanded. "The owners aren't home, so you can't come in. If they come home and see you, they'll think I brought you and that I'm stealing stuff. You need to wait outside."

I was confused, but I sat down on the sidewalk and waited for her to finish work. As I sat there, I thought about my mother potentially being accused of stealing and realized this was humiliating and demeaning work for her. It wasn't right that she was someone else's servant, so when she came out to see me a short time later, I told her, "Mom, I don't want you to do that job anymore."

"Look," she said, "we just came to America. If I don't have a job, we'll waste all our savings. I need a job to pay our bills."

It was summer vacation, so I wasn't in school and didn't have much to do for the next two months. "I'll get a job," I told her. "You can stop working tomorrow." The next day, I went around the area knocking on people's doors and offering to clean their yards for five dollars an hour. I got lots of work, and I worked hard. I gave most of that money to my mother.

At the end of one day, I came home after pulling weeds with scratches all over my hands and barbs stuck in my skin. As she cleaned up my hands, my mother began to cry. She felt guilty that her son's hands were torn to shreds so that she wouldn't have to work, but I told her it was OK because I wasn't going to do yard work anymore. I'd found a new job working for a Hungarian Jewish couple named Manyos and Jerry, who owned a small restaurant in West Hollywood.

The couple were Holocaust survivors, and they told me the most horrendous stories of living under Nazi occupation and in the Nazi concentration camp when she was eighteen and he was nineteen. To escape, they hid in the sewers.

"You see my wife here?" Jerry asked me one day, holding his wife's hand. "She was in the sewer lines with me. The sewage was up to here." He brought his free hand up to my chin. "We were swimming in it alongside the rats, and we could barely breathe. But she was strong. 'Don't give up, Jerry,' she told me. 'Don't give up. We will make it.' And we did. That's why we're here, because of her."

Manyos and Jerry stayed in the sewers for weeks, hiding from the Nazis and going from one area to another until, miraculously, they made it safely out. Tears rolled down his face as he told me their story. I'd never seen two people so closely connected and who had shared so much terror and pain. After the war, they moved to Israel and then to America. Like thousands of others, they had tried to make the world a better place and put the horrors of the war behind them.

My shift at the restaurant started at 7:00 a.m., when I helped Manyos prepare the day's food and do whatever else needed to be done. My respect for this couple grew stronger every day, and I was awestruck by their stories of survival and perseverance. At the same time, I was shaken to my very soul that people could be so cruel to one another and that they could treat their fellow human beings with such hatred. I cried with them when they told me their stories, and I loved them like they were my own parents.

I learned more about running a restaurant from Manyos and Jerry than I had learned working at my mother's place in Tel Aviv. Their restaurant was just a standard diner, but it always had lines of people waiting on the street to get in because they had cracked the secret recipe of success. It wasn't that hard: they served good, fresh food at a reasonable price in a clean place.

Watching Manyos and Jerry with admiration, I was proud to see the money rolling in for them, but I also realized that what they were doing wasn't difficult if you knew the secret recipe. I wanted a piece of the action, and I wanted to emulate what they had achieved. Inspired by them, I knew I could also make good money if I put my mind to it.

CHAPTER 6

BURGER JOINT

Working for Manyos and Jerry inspired me to start looking for my own restaurant to run. I hadn't even turned sixteen yet, but I was confident I knew enough to run a successful restaurant like theirs. Hot dog places and burger joints were all over Los Angeles, and a lot of them were really successful. The most famous was Pink's, which was not far from my parents' house in the Fairfax District. Pink's was the model for everything I wanted. Betty and Paul Pink started the business in 1939, selling hot dogs from a cart on a rented piece of land. They eventually bought the land and built a small restaurant, which is still in operation and is still called Pink's.

The Pinks didn't invent the hot dog stand or the burger joint, but Pink's is the model for other restaurants of this type. Inside, there was a counter and a few small tables. Outside, there was always a line. It wouldn't be an iconic Los Angeles landmark and people wouldn't keep coming back unless it served great food and gave customers a great experience. It's a phenomenon that I haven't seen anywhere else. You can drive past Pink's at any time of the day or night—whether it's 2:00 p.m. or 2:00 a.m.—and there is always a line of people waiting to order.

A lot of restaurants like Pink's opened in the 1930s and 1940s, and they became the standard for local diners. They all had a grill, ovens, a deep fryer, a three-compartment sink, and a toilet in the back. It seemed like almost every movie that was set in Los Angeles in this era had a scene in a diner like this.

One day in 1975, soon after I got my learner's permit, I was driving in downtown Los Angeles when I noticed that a restaurant on the corner of South Los Angeles Street and East Pico Boulevard had recently closed. It looked a lot like the one Manyos and Jerry owned. There was no sign saying it was for rent, but I found the landlord, who was a big clothing whole-saler. I told him I wanted to rent his space.

"Is it available?" I asked him.

"Yeah," he said, "it's available. And you want to rent it? How old are you?"

"Eighteen," I said . . . convincingly.

"Why do you want to rent it?" he asked, probably thinking I was trying to prank him. I told him I knew how to run a burger joint and that I wanted to set up a good business.

"Are you going to do this by yourself?" he asked me. I lied again and explained that our family had recently moved here from Israel and that I was actually trying to find a restaurant for my uncle, who didn't speak English. It would be my uncle's restaurant, but I would help him. He seemed even more skeptical, but I arranged to bring my uncle by to meet him at the restaurant the next day.

* * *

At that point, I had to make a choice: commit to opening the business or go back to school. I was only a sophomore at Hollywood High, so dropping out would be a pretty gutsy thing to do. I could hire someone to run the restaurant while I went to school, but what would be the point of doing that if I wasn't going to be in charge and make it my own business?

I had always been resourceful and managed to have some cash in my pocket from working odd jobs and trading things, but I certainly didn't have the kind of money required to sign a lease for a burger joint in downtown Los Angeles, let alone fix it up and order all the supplies I needed to get it up and running. I figured it would take about $5,000 to pay the initial rent and get the place cleaned up and ready for business, but I was determined to find the money somewhere. In 1975, however, $5,000 was more money than most people had lying around—even if they *were* willing to take a chance and give it to an almost-sixteen-year-old kid with a dream.

That night, I sat down with my parents at the breakfast nook in the kitchen and told them I was opening a business and wasn't going back to school. I didn't know how they would react. At first, they told me not to do it, insisting that I was too young to leave school and that I needed to get an education. Although they were successful in their own lives, they were high school dropouts themselves, and they'd had to fight for everything. They'd gotten married when my mother was sixteen, which was only a few months older than I was at that time, and they knew this would be tough for me.

Over the course of the evening, I managed to convince them that this was the right decision. I told them it was a great opportunity that would never come along again, and I promised them I would go back to school later when things were less hectic.

If my parents had gone to college, I think it would have been harder for them to accept the fact that their son wanted to drop out of high school as a sophomore and start his own business. They wanted me to have a better life than they'd had and not make the same mistakes they had made. The path they saw for me was graduating from high school and then university—the same path that millions of other parents across America envisioned for their children. Deep down, though, they knew that what I planned to do was no different from what they had done in Jerusalem thirty-four years earlier.

For my parents and for most Israelis their age, life was about survival. Many were Holocaust survivors, and everyone knew people who'd been in concentration camps. As one example, my brother-in-law's parents had been in concentration camps when they were young, so they'd never had the chance to go to school. Their youth was spent trying to survive. My parents understood (although most of today's families would *not* understand) that when you find an opportunity like the one I had, you should take it. It's always possible to get an education later.

Once the matter of school was settled, we moved on to the topic of money. When I told them I thought it would take $5,000 to set up the business, I could see that they knew where this was going. They thought about it for a couple of minutes, but neither of them said anything. My mother got up and went over to the refrigerator to find something to drink, then she came back to the breakfast nook and leaned in toward me. She whispered in my ear, "Do the best you can. I'll talk to your father."

Even after buying the house in the Fairfax District—which cost around $90,000—my father still had some money saved. Even though $5,000 was a significant amount of money in 1975, my father always trusted me, and he agreed to lend me what I needed. I was ready to make my mark in the world.

* * *

Downtown Los Angeles wasn't particularly distinctive in 1975, especially compared to a skyline like New York City's. Today, downtown LA is home to world-renowned destinations such as Frank Gehry's Walt Disney Concert Hall, the Cathedral of Our Lady of the Angels, and the Museum of Contemporary Art, as well as Crypto.com Arena (also known as the Staples Center), home of the Los Angeles Lakers and the Clippers professional basketball teams. None of these buildings was there in 1975. Even the Lakers—led by Wilt Chamberlain and Jerry

West—played miles away in Inglewood at The Forum.

For much of the twentieth century, what downtown Los Angeles had going for it was shopping, movie theaters, and live shows. Several blocks around Broadway and Seventh Street were home to elegant department stores such as Hamburger's (which later became May Company), Bullock's, The Broadway, Harris & Frank, and J. W. Robinson's. These stores were among the greatest showplaces for the best goods America had to offer, and they were a destination for generations of Angelenos—but they were starting to decline in importance by the late 1960s and 1970s.

Starting in the 1930s, many of the beautiful older buildings in downtown LA were demolished to create parking lots. Even then, the automobile was becoming king in Southern California, and the destruction of downtown residential areas forced people out into the greater metropolitan area, helping turn downtown Los Angeles into a place where people drove to for work or entertainment but drove away from at the end of the day.

Until the late 1950s, there was a thirteen-story height limit on buildings in downtown Los Angeles. But by the time I got there, the new downtown area in nearby Bunker Hill was in a building boom. City blocks were being cleared so new skyscrapers could go up, and many of the high-rise buildings in the historic downtown were becoming vacant as people and businesses moved to the new skyscrapers and the suburbs. Department stores and movie theaters were built in places such as West Hollywood and Beverly Hills, so people didn't need to go downtown anymore for shopping and movies.

Los Angeles's modern skyline was starting to take shape. The United California Bank Building (now known as the Aon Center) had been open for only about a year and was the tallest building in downtown until 1989. Other recently completed buildings such as Security Pacific Plaza (now the Bank of America Plaza) and the twin Bank of America and ARCO towers (now City National and Paul Hastings towers), along with the elegant and distinctive Los Angeles City Hall, gave downtown a sense of identity that it had lacked before.

The burger joint I was hoping to open was in the part of historic downtown once known as the Garment District but now becoming known as the Fashion District. Covering just a few square miles, the Fashion District was home to literally hundreds of garment manufacturers and small retail and wholesale businesses, most of which sold fabrics, clothing, and footwear.

If you'd asked the average Angeleno in 1975 where the Fashion District was, you would have been met with blank stares. It wasn't somewhere the average person ever went, except to drive through to get to somewhere else, but the wholesale clothing industry and movie industry knew all about it. The fashions were great, and people came from Paris, Milan, London, and all over the world to shop there.

The Fashion District bordered the central downtown area and a fifty-block area known as Skid Row. Everyone had heard of Skid Row, which was synonymous with homelessness. Since the late 1800s, it had been a low-rent area where transients and seasonal laborers congregated. By the early years of the Great Depression in the 1930s, there might have been as many as ten thousand homeless people living on the streets. Skid Row might be considered the beginning of the homeless problem that has plagued Los Angeles to this day.

Skid Row is still home to what has been described as possibly the largest "stable" population of homeless people in the United States, which seems like a contradiction but makes sense if you've ever driven through the area and seen what looks like permanent homeless encampments. Back in the mid-1970s, many of the homeless were Vietnam War veterans. Services and missions catered to the homeless and the hungry, and numerous charities and civic-minded individuals spent time and effort helping the people there; the most famous volunteers were a former nun, Catherine Morris, and her husband, Jeff Dietrich, who founded the Hippie Kitchen to assist the downtrodden.

* * *

After convincing the restaurant owner to meet me and my uncle the next day, and having convinced my father to lend me $5,000, I just needed to find an "uncle" to bring with me. Luckily, I had a real uncle who'd just moved from Israel to Los Angeles. I told him I was trying to rent a space to open a burger joint, and he agreed to come with me. I told him just to nod and shake his head for "Yes" and "No" but to leave the talking to me. I would translate into Hebrew to keep the ruse alive.

I'm sure the owner realized what I was doing and that I wasn't eighteen, but he had a good property that was sitting empty while he was losing money, and I was willing to sign a lease and hand over the first and last months' rent, so what did he care who it was really for? It didn't take long for us to sign the paperwork, and I ended up leasing the space for $500 a month.

Other than my own family, the first people I told about my new lease were Manyos and Jerry. I was a little afraid of quitting my job at their restaurant and letting them down, but they were really happy for me. They were proud that I was moving on and were thrilled to see a young kid succeeding. They had witnessed the worst that mankind had to offer, and they knew the antidote was love, encouragement, and support. They genuinely wanted the next generation to do better.

My burger joint was located on a busy street with lots of people coming and going, and I knew that people on the move always needed a good, clean place to eat. I also wanted to catch the attention of some of the shoppers on their way into and out of downtown LA.

The restaurant was set up as a classic Los Angeles diner, with stools at the counter and a few tables and booths. It had promise, but the equipment was old and beat-up, and it hadn't been cleaned for a long time—probably years. The walls in the kitchen were coated with grease, and the hood over the grill that was supposed to vent the smoke and grease outside was so clogged that it barely worked. But I could see beyond the oil and grime. All it needed was a good cleaning and someone with vision to take it over.

The first thing I did was thoroughly clean the place and then replace the old broken fixtures with new ones. My beloved brothers Abe and Jacob now owned a huge garage that did automobile repairs. They worked at the garage from 7:00 a.m. to 5:00 p.m., but as soon as they were done, Abe would come to my restaurant and help me clean and paint. He was with me until 9:00 p.m. most nights. I also hired a few people to help me clean the equipment. The cleaning and renovation took about six weeks, and then I was open for business.

Manyos and Jerry had taught me how to cook and run a grill, but I knew I wouldn't have time to do everything. So the first person I hired was a cook named Vincent. He walked in off the street one day while we were cleaning and asked if I needed a cook. He said he could cook Mexican and American food, so I told him to come back and start work in a week when we opened.

Vincent was more than double my age, probably in his thirties or early forties. To some people, it might seem strange or uncomfortable having a boss who was so much younger signing their paychecks, but to me it seemed natural. When you're not quite sixteen, everyone you hire is going to be older, so I never gave it much thought.

My typical day at the burger joint started at 3:30 or 4:00 a.m. I would drive to downtown LA, park the car, walk into my restaurant, and get to work. I didn't have my full driver's license yet, meaning I was supposed to have an adult in the car with me whenever I was behind the wheel, but I drove by myself anyway. It would be a couple more months until I got my full license.

The first thing I did each morning was to make sure the restaurant was clean. I've been a clean freak ever since I was a child, and I'm still a clean freak in my home and businesses. Burger joints have a stereotype of being dirty, but mine never were. There's a saying that the dirtier the kitchen, the better the food—because supposedly the owners put all their effort into the food. I've never bought into that idea. A dirty kitchen is a terrible place to work, and it attracts vermin and bugs. It takes a little extra effort to keep it clean, but people notice a sparkling kitchen.

By 5:00 a.m., I was ready to start receiving deliveries, and then I started helping the cook prepare for the breakfast crowd. When breakfast was over, we'd start preparing for lunch. The downtown area had a lot of people coming and going during the day, especially in the Fashion District. Things slowed down a lot in the afternoon, though, because most people lived outside downtown and drove home after work. After 5:00 p.m., it was a ghost town. Most days, I shut the place down at 4:30 or 5:00 p.m. Before I went home, I washed and cleaned the whole restaurant, which took about an hour, so I was there from 4:00 a.m. to 5:00 or 6:00 p.m. every day, thirteen or fourteen hours straight. I would never have had time for high school!

My lifestyle certainly wasn't typical for a kid my age. My

friends and cousins were off doing things in the evenings and on weekends, but I needed to keep my business going. They went to the beach and to parties and movies, and they also saw some of the great 1970s bands that I loved—Pink Floyd, Paul McCartney and Wings, Elton John, Electric Light Orchestra, the Rolling Stones, Queen, and Deep Purple—in concert. And there were so many movies—*Jaws, One Flew over the Cuckoo's Nest, Rocky*—that I didn't get to see in the theaters when they came out. I missed out on all that—which I still regret because I would have loved to have been part of that experience—but I made up for it later and eventually saw all the bands and all the movies.

I wasn't even sixteen yet, and I wasn't legally allowed to drive by myself, but the burger joint in downtown Los Angeles was mine. I'd built it up from nothing, but I never bragged about it and I never showed off. When friends came by, I never let them know I owned it. They thought I was working for my parents or my brothers.

It all seemed worth the sacrifice. The restaurant was a success. People loved the food, and I had a steady business all day long. I was happy and I was making money.

CHAPTER 7

AUTO SHOPS

B usiness was great at my burger joint, and less than a year after it opened, I got an offer I couldn't turn down. The broker for the building came in one day and told me that a young Korean family was willing to buy me out for $25,000. The main reason they wanted my restaurant was that it would allow them to invest at least $10,000 in a business, which would create an easier path for them to become legal permanent residents in the US. Since my burger joint was already established and a proven success, they thought it was a good opportunity.

I accepted the $25,000 offer and sold the burger joint. After I paid back my father the $5,000 I had borrowed from him, along with a few other expenses, I was left with about an $18,000 profit. Not bad for a sixteen-year-old kid who'd dropped out of high school!

While the sale was going through, I drove down South Los Angeles Street and noticed another old beat-up burger joint that was being run by an old couple on the corner of South Los

Angeles Street and West Olympic Boulevard. It reminded me of how my burger joint looked before I fixed it up, so I went in and offered to buy it for $6,000. The couple was ready to retire, and they were happy to sell it to me.

So I started all over again, just three blocks north of my original burger joint. It took me another $6,000 to fix it up, but I did the same thing as before—cleaned it, got it running, and made it a success.

Less than six months later, I sold that restaurant for $25,000 to another Korean family. I had doubled my investment in less than six months, and I was feeling pretty good about my choices. A few days later, I found another old burger joint that had been run by another old couple, and I managed to buy it for about $5,000. This place was another three blocks north on South Los Angeles Street, at Seventh Street. I spent about $6,000 to fix it up, and I sold it as well a few months later for $30,000.

At the age of eighteen, I was riding high. I had opened and sold three popular burger joints and had $40,000 in the bank. I also bought a fourth burger joint, but I set that one up for my sister and her husband, who were immigrating from Israel. They liked the idea of what I was doing, and they made a good living from it for ten years before they moved on to other ventures. The main reason I didn't get involved in that restaurant was that fate intervened and produced a fork in the road, and I eagerly headed out in a new direction.

AUTO SHOPS

* * *

In October 1978, I was nineteen years old and had very little to do. I was bored and drove around a lot. Not too far from my parents' house, I noticed an old gas station on the corner of West Boulevard and West Pico Boulevard with a sign that said, "For Sale or Lease." It was in a nice part of town in an upscale neighborhood, Victoria Park, close to downtown Los Angeles and Hollywood. The neighborhood had been established in the early 1900s with beautiful houses built in the American Arts and Crafts style.

I have always been obsessed with cars and motorcycles. From the age of ten or eleven, I had been a car freak. My family owned a Chevy Impala—a standard, unexciting, middle-class car—but whenever I walked or rode my bike past an attractive car that was parked next to the sidewalk, I spent several minutes examining every detail. I checked out the speedometer to see how fast it could go, looked at the interior to see if it was made of leather, and examined the paint job, bumpers, and every other detail.

My absolute favorite cars were the big American muscle cars. I was just the right age at just the right time in history, because muscle cars had a pretty short lifespan from the mid-1960s to the early 1970s. In 1969, when I was ten years old, muscle cars were in their heyday, and they were the only cars I really cared about. Some kids were obsessed with baseball or soccer, but for me, it was American muscle cars. Ferraris and Lamborghinis were nice, but I didn't know much about them—and I would have taken a muscle car over a Lamborghini any day of the week.

Muscle cars were American two-door sports coupes with powerful engines, usually V8s. They were sleek and beautiful, and I dreamed about driving them as fast as they could go. The most famous muscle cars were the Chevrolet Corvette, the Dodge Charger R/T, the Ford Mustang, the Buick GSX, the Chevrolet Chevelle, and the Plymouth Hemi Cuda convertible. There weren't a lot of these cars in Tel Aviv when I was a kid, but whenever I found one, I felt like I'd hit the jackpot.

The Clean Air Act, oil crisis, and skyrocketing insurance prices brought the era of muscle cars to an end about the time I arrived in Los Angeles in 1973. That didn't stop my love affair with cars, so when I saw the "For Sale or Lease" sign at the old gas station on the corner, I started having visions of how I could turn my passion for cars into a business.

I had an idea of what I wanted to do, so I called the guy listed on the sign, Alan Riseman from La Mancha Development Corporation, and told him I wanted to lease the building. Alan was an older Jewish guy and a Holocaust survivor, and he was the owner of the property. When he met me, he realized right away from my accent that I was an Israeli. He also saw that I was young.

"What do you want to do with this, kid?" Alan asked me.

"I've always dreamed of opening up my own auto mechanic shop," I told him.

"And you want to lease it?"

"Yeah. I want to lease it and turn it into something."

"Can I give you some advice, from a father to a son?" he asked me.

"Of course," I replied.

"Don't ever lease. Every opportunity you have to buy, buy it." This turned out to be the best advice I ever received in my life, and it has guided my career ever since.

I had no idea what the property might be worth, but I was sure it was quite a bit more than the $40,000 I had in the bank. It never even crossed my mind that I could buy this property, but I asked Alan how much he wanted for it.

"Do you have any money saved?" he asked. I told him I had a little more than $40,000.

"Well, I'll tell you what I'm going to do for you," he said. "I'm going to sell it to you for $90,000. You give me $30,000, and I'll carry you for $60,000 at 10 percent interest for two years. After two years, you bring me the balance." Interest rates from the bank in 1978 were about 10 percent and rising, so it was a fair offer.

And so I bought the gas station. The paperwork was recorded by Los Angeles County on November 13, 1978, and, at age nineteen, I owned the old gas station. I spent my remaining $10,000 fixing up the property and buying the right equipment, and not long afterward I opened my first auto shop. With my love for cars, it was the perfect fit for me.

To be honest, restaurants never meant that much to me.

They weren't my passion, but I had the experience from my mother's restaurant in Tel Aviv and my brother's restaurant in Pomona. So when the opportunities to run my own burger joints came my way, I took them. I was a young guy, and I'd found a way to make a living. But the restaurants were a means to an end, and I never regretted getting out of that business. In less than three years in the burger business, I had put $40,000 in my pocket, which gave me the freedom to move on to the next step.

Working with cars, though, was something different. It was something I cared about. It was more than just the money.

* * *

The strange thing is that even though I loved cars, I didn't know much about them. I had a basic understanding of how they worked, but I was not a mechanic. The thing I knew best was how to hire the right people, so I hired a couple of great mechanics. It was the same with the burger joints—I wasn't a chef, but I knew how to hire great chefs. And I knew how to run a business.

The best mechanics I knew were my brothers Abe and Jacob, but by then they already owned a successful automobile shop of their own—a huge operation on Melrose Avenue, a couple of miles away. My cousin Yoni was also a great mechanic. He arrived in Los Angeles not long after I got there and was looking for work, so I hired him.

Los Angeles in the late 1970s was the automobile center

of the world. Everyone had a car, and most households had more than one. The city was so spread out and everything was so far away that without a car it was impossible to do anything or go anywhere. About one out of every thirty-five cars in the entire US was in Los Angeles County, so there was no shortage of customers.

Every one of those cars had to be worked on at some time or another. Cars were always breaking down and people were always getting into wrecks and fender-benders, plus the cars needed oil changes and tune-ups. I just had to show that I was doing good work and that my auto shop was better than the others, and people would bring me their business. It didn't take long for word to get around, and I soon had all the business I could handle.

In addition to the mechanic shop, I added a body shop on the side of the main building. That way, I could work on the engines and get the dents and scratches out at the same time. My brothers were great mechanics, but they didn't do body-work. Whenever anyone came in with a car that needed body-work, they knew they could send the business my way.

* * *

Just as we were about to close the shop one Friday afternoon, a guy drove up in a nice two-door Mercedes convertible. He knew my brothers from when they'd all lived in Tel Aviv, and he had been to their auto shop to see if they could get a dent out of his front fender. Since my brothers didn't do bodywork, they sent him to me, thinking they were doing me a favor.

"I hear you do good work," he said.

"Yeah," I told him as I looked over the damage to his car, "but we're closing. I'll get it done for you by Tuesday."

What I didn't know at the time was that this guy was Micky Levine, a gangster and drug dealer. He was the perfect gangster—ruthless and without remorse. The way he carried himself and the way he flashed hundred dollar bills should have tipped me off that he was not someone I could trust and not someone I wanted to get involved with.

"Tomorrow," he said as walked toward one of his associates, a thug named Vince, who'd followed him to my shop in another car. "I want it tomorrow." The way he said it, it was like he was threatening me. I never liked being told what to do, especially by someone with no respect for other people, so I repeated that I could get it done by Tuesday.

"I don't think you heard me," he said as he turned around and got right up in my face. "I need it tomorrow."

"The best I can do is late on Monday," I said. "You want it done right?" He didn't say anything, but he drove away with a scowl on his face and a look in his eyes that could kill. He was not used to having anyone stand up to him, let alone a cocky kid, but he was desperate to get his car fixed.

Later, I learned the reason Micky wanted the job done so quickly was that he'd allegedly used the car as a battering-ram to stop one of his low-level drug dealers from getting away. The guy owed him some money and was trying to escape down an alley. Micky chased after him in his car and deliberately hit him, and now Micky was anxious to cover up the evidence.

At the end of the day on Monday, Vince dropped by to pick up the car, and all was good. That is, until I got word that Micky was ranting to my brothers that we had done a terrible job and was making threats against me. I knew we did good work, and the car looked as good as new to me, so I called over my bodywork guy, Carlos, to find out what the problem was. It turned out that Carlos had gotten behind over the weekend and cut some corners. He painted around the bumper instead of taking it off first, and one of Micky's guys noticed. Micky was right—it was a botched job.

I knew I'd messed up, so I called Micky right away to apologize and to offer to redo the job—but instead of being reasonable, he was steamed and made all sorts of threats against me, most of which involved killing me in the most unpleasant ways. The way he reacted, it was like I'd killed his brother or stolen $1 million from him. The car would have been easy to fix, but I didn't like the threats Micky was making or the way he was talking to me. I got into a shouting match with him before he made more threats and slammed down the phone.

I didn't take his threats seriously—I'd heard them all before, especially in my brother's casino in Tel Aviv—but it took me a couple of days to realize what deep shit I'd landed myself in. That's when my brothers told me who Micky really was and that he was probably stressed out over a drug deal that went wrong. They also let me know that he was known to follow up on his threats and had no problem getting rid of people he didn't like. I'd heard about a couple who checked into the Biltmore Hotel in Los Angeles but left the hotel stuffed into their own luggage. Allegedly, they'd double-crossed Micky at some point, and he'd had them killed. Someone else who Micky didn't like was Tommy Goldberg—the guy who shot Abe in the head in Tel Aviv. Micky and Tommy once had a dispute over a girlfriend, and Micky had ordered a hit on Tommy.

I kept telling myself that this was just a minor repair gone wrong, but my gut told me things would only get worse. "So what do I do now?" I asked my brothers.

"Just lie low. We'll do what we can to smooth things out," Jacob told me. It wasn't very reassuring, but it was the only thing I could do.

Luckily for me, Micky left for a "business trip" to Tel Aviv for a few days, so I was hoping everything would calm down by the time he got back.

The next day, Yoni came up to me at work with a huge grin on his face. "You are the luckiest son of a bitch I know," he said. "I've got some fantastic news. Micky Levine is dead. He got popped in Tel Aviv last night."

All of a sudden, the weight of the world was lifted from my shoulders. I hate to profit from other people's misfortune, but Micky was the exception. Besides, it's not like I stole from him or did him any harm. He simply overreacted and lashed out, which is no doubt why he got killed in Tel Aviv. Things had been looking grim, but now I had no worries and could get back to doing what I knew best.

* * *

After about two years of running my own auto shop, fate intervened again when I noticed a new trend in Los Angeles. People were building auto bays—sort of like a strip mall, but each of the small independent shops was specialized in one part of the automobile business. Someone was a mechanic, someone else did bodywork, and others did upholstery, installed music systems, did custom paint jobs, and so on. Each was a separate business, but together they made a one-stop shop for everything a car owner could need.

One of these auto bays had opened nearby on Pico Boulevard, so I talked to the guy who owned it. He told me he was charging $1,200 rent per bay per month. I started wondering how that compared to what I was making. My mechanic shop and body shop brought in about $25,000 a month, but I had employees to pay and a lot of other expenses, plus it took a lot of my time. Still, I'd managed to save some money, and I'd paid off the balance of my loan from Alan Riseman, so I owned the property outright and could do what I wanted with it.

I decided to do what this guy on Pico Boulevard did. I demolished my auto shop and built ten auto bays on the property. The rent for each bay was $1,500 a month, and my net profit from rent was $10,000 a month. Best of all, I was still in the automobile business.

This was 1981; I was twenty-one years old, and I'd already moved from owning three burger joints and an auto mechanic and body shop to being a landlord. Once my new business proved to be successful, I found another corner location, bought it, and converted it into more auto bays. When that business was built up, I refinanced it and used the money to buy another corner lot that also became auto bays—and I ended up with four different locations across Los Angeles by the time I was twenty-four.

I was fortunate that every business I opened was a success—but it was more than just luck and more than just reaping the rewards of hard work and passion. There's no magic formula and there's no guarantee of success, but I believe a major factor in my success is that I've always been conservative with money and have always been fair and honest. I don't like to take unnecessary risks, so I never took out more than 50 percent of the value of one property to finance the next one. That way, I was never overleveraged and could quickly recover if anything ever went bad. Fortunately, nothing ever went bad. In fact, just the opposite.

CHAPTER 8

ALINE

One day in January 1980 while I was sitting in my office in my auto shop, my brother Jacob called me from his shop a few miles away.

"I'm sending someone over to you," he told me. "A really gorgeous young girl. She rear-ended someone with her Ford Granada, and she needs her hood fixed before I can get to the engine. I told her to ask for you."

A short time later, the most stunning young woman drove up in a Ford Granada and asked to see Izek. She was even better looking than Jacob had made her out to be. "I'm Izek," I introduced myself.

"Hi," she said. "Your brother sent me. I can't get my hood open. Can you help me?" I was bowled over by her beauty as I stammered out that we could fix her hood but that it would take half an hour. I'd never seen anyone so charming and elegant, and I didn't know how to act around her.

I called over to Enrique, a worker in the body shop, and

told him to take a look at the car. I was always shy around girls, and I'd never really had a girlfriend. I don't know where I got the courage, but as Enrique was looking at the hood, I asked her, "Do you want to grab a coffee across the street while your car gets fixed?"

She agreed, so we went across the road to the coffee shop. A short time later, we walked back to the body shop and she asked how much she owed me. I told her not to worry about it, but she insisted, so I told her just to tip Enrique.

I supposed I had been flirting with her the entire time, and as she was walking out, I asked her for her phone number. I'd never done anything like that before, especially with someone so beautiful. She hesitated.

"I can't give you my phone number because my father is very strict," she said. I felt defeated and a little embarrassed, but before I could say anything she added, "But I'll give you the number of the store where I work." Back then, long before the luxury of cell phones, the only way to call someone was on a home or business line. She worked part-time at the Yves Saint Laurent Rive Gauche boutique in Beverly Hills, and she gave me a business card for the store. "You can call me there," she said.

She started to drive off, but she stopped a few feet later, rolled down the window, and asked me to give her back the business card. I was shocked and devastated, but then she wrote another number on the card. "That's my home phone," she said. "You can call me." I was on top of the world.

I really wanted to call her that evening, but I waited a couple of days before calling the home number she'd written on the card. Someone picked up the phone and I asked, "Can I speak to Aline, please?"

"This is Aline."

"Hi, Aline, this is Izek."

"Who?"

"Izek."

"How can I help you, Izek?"

"Are you Aline Wizmann?"

"Yes."

"It seems like you don't remember me," I said. "You came to my auto shop two days ago."

"I've never been to your auto shop."

I was crestfallen when I realized the girl who had come to my shop had already forgotten about Izek from the body shop. I apologized for disturbing whoever this was on the phone and was about to hang up when she said, "Wait a minute. Maybe you were talking to my cousin."

"Is your cousin also named Aline?" I asked.

"Yes."

"Aline Wizmann?"

"Yes. Hold on. I'll get her."

It turned out that Aline's cousin was also named Aline. Their mothers were sisters, and their fathers were brothers named Wizmann—and they both called their daughters Aline. That's how I got my first date with Aline, and it's all history since then. I am not particularly religious, but I believe this was a trick played by God to get us together and to guide us in the right direction.

* * *

I was twenty years old when I met Aline. She was eighteen, and the first thing that attracted me to her was her striking looks. At that age, that's all you think about! You don't think about what the future might look like and that you might eventually settle down with someone. I was more concerned with trying to get my business established and having fun with my cousins and friends than finding a future wife.

Aline's parents lived near my parents' house. For our first date, I drove over and picked her up in my burgundy Corvette, which was my pride and joy. I suppose I was trying to show off a little, which I'd never done before, especially around girls. But I'd never met anyone like Aline, and I didn't know the proper etiquette for taking a girl out. We stopped for a bite to eat at a small restaurant that was owned by one of my friends before we went to see the Francis Ford Coppola movie *Apocalypse Now* at a theater in Hollywood. That was quite an intense movie for a first date, but I'd seen it before and really loved it.

After the movie, we stopped at a 7-Eleven on Sunset Boulevard to get some chocolate bars and a couple of Cokes. In those days, a lot of prostitutes worked Sunset Boulevard, and as we were standing in line at the 7-Eleven, the beautiful girl in front of us asked the cashier for a pack of Marlboro cigarettes and a pack of condoms. I was taken aback by how casual and open she was, and I whispered to Aline what I'd just heard. Her eyes grew wide, and I think she might have blushed.

When it was my turn to pay, I put the chocolate bars and the Cokes on the counter and started joking with the cashier about how brazen the girl was in asking for condoms—and how many she might use that night. Then I said, "Oh, and give me a pack of condoms." It was said as an innocent joke, but as soon as those words left my mouth, I realized Aline would be offended. Here we were on our first date and I was asking for condoms! I immediately apologized and told her it was just something I'd blurted out. Luckily for me, she didn't think I was being aggressive or presumptuous, and she laughed along with the cashier at my stumbling awkwardness.

When I dropped Aline off at home that night, I gave her a kiss on the cheek. After the second date, I gave her another kiss on the cheek. I was a gentleman with her, and it wasn't until our fourth date that we kissed on the lips. I respected her, and she loved that I treated her well. She still tells our children about this and how important it is to be treated like a lady.

* * *

Aline grew up in Paris, France, but she moved to Israel in 1971 when she was ten years old and came to America with her parents in 1978 when she was seventeen. When I met her, she had just graduated from Fairfax High School in Los Angeles. In addition to working in the boutique in Beverly Hills, she was going to Los Angeles Valley College in the San Fernando Valley.

At first, Aline's parents didn't think I was right for her. Like many parents, they dreamed of their beautiful young daughter marrying a doctor or an attorney or an engineer, but I was just a young kid who was working in an auto shop. At the beginning, I never told Aline that I owned the business. I let her think it was my father's business and that I was running it. I was humble about it, and it wasn't until several months later that I told her the truth. She knew that I'd dropped out of high school and owned some property, but she never knew that I'd owned all those burger joints and that I owned the auto shop.

After only a couple of months, I knew Aline was the only one for me. Yes, it was her beauty that first caught my eye, but all the other pieces fell into place quickly. I'd never connected with someone the way I connected with her, and I'd never given much thought to my own future, but suddenly I wanted a future with Aline. I was head over heels in love.

I was still living in a room at the back of my parents' house on Crescent Heights Boulevard and, after about six months, Aline and I decided to rent a one-bedroom apartment and move in together. Even though we hadn't told my parents, my mother must have figured it out because she came up to Aline the next day and told her, "I need my son at home. Please do not take him." Aline was upset and came to me crying, so I told my mother that while it was true I was moving out, I was twenty and it was time for me to leave. On the day I moved my stuff out of my parents' house, my mother watched with tears in her eyes, but that was also the day she understood it was the right thing to do. She told Aline that she loved her and gave us her blessing.

In December 1983, with my business going well, I proposed to Aline. We got married in May 1984 in a huge wedding with about five hundred guests.

I bought my first house a couple of years before we got married. We lived there until 1984, when I bought a bigger house in Mount Olympus, a spectacular area in the Hollywood Hills between Laurel Canyon and Runyon Canyon. We moved into that house as a couple, and we lived there for fourteen years and had five babies: Eric in 1984, Sara in 1986, Jonathan in 1988, Jessica in 1990, and Jimmy in 1993.

It was always my dream to have a lot of children, but at first, Aline did not want as many as I did. She said she would be happy with just one—but once Eric was born, she changed her mind. She realized what a great gift children are and what joy they bring to your life. When we had Jimmy, our fifth child, in 1993, I had just turned thirty-four and she was almost thirty-two, and it seemed like five kids was the right number for us.

* * *

One of the many things I've always loved about Aline is that she's very friendly. She talks to everyone, from the homeless to royalty, and she loves to give compliments. She even stops people on the street to tell them how wonderful they look. The best thing is that every word out of her mouth is genuine, and she never looks for compliments in return. She proudly tells people that she and I have been together for so long because we have the highest respect for each other.

Family has always been important to Aline and me. When I look around, I see so many people who live flashy lifestyles but have empty lives. I have read too many stories of people who drift into depression and are unhappy because they have forgotten what gave them success in the first place and what family really means to them. Money can have a terrible, destructive effect on a person, but I can honestly say I have never fallen into that trap.

Although Aline has never had a full-time job outside the home, she has always helped me in my business. When I was building houses and apartments, once the kids started going to school, she often assisted in the leasing office and came up with ideas for furniture and appliances and decor to help make the places more attractive for tenants. She is a valuable asset to the business, and I have never been shy about giving her the credit she deserves.

Even after all these years, Aline and I are still devoted to each other. We've even made a pact. Whoever dies first and goes to wherever it is we go—heaven or hell or someplace else—will wait at the gates of that place until the other one arrives. We'll be with each other for eternity.

* * *

In my entire life, I have never defaulted on a loan or even missed a loan payment—except for one $10,000 loan that I have never repaid.

When Aline was working in the boutique in Beverly Hills after she graduated from high school, she'd managed to save about $7,000 in cash and owned the Ford Granada she drove to my shop on the day I met her. The car was worth $3,500.

The deal I'd made with Alan Riseman to buy the old gas station that became my auto mechanic body shop was that I'd give him $30,000 and would repay him the remaining $60,000 plus interest two years later. About a year after I started dating Aline, the two-year deadline was approaching, and I needed to find the money to repay Alan.

Even with my own savings and the money I was able to raise from my father and brothers, I was still about $10,000 short. I knew that Aline had a little money saved, so I explained the situation to her, then I told her, "I'm embarrassed to ask, but I know you have some money. If you can lend it to me, I'll give you whatever collateral you want, even my Corvette."

"You don't have to give me anything," she said. "I trust you." And she handed me $7,000 in cash and let me sell her car for $3,500. She kept $500, and from then onward we shared my Corvette.

I paid Alan what I owed him, and I paid back my father and

my brothers. But up until this day, I have never paid Aline back her $10,000 (I tried, but she wouldn't let me), despite the fact that it was one of the most timely and consequential loans in my entire career. With the loan to Alan paid off, I was solidly on the path to living the American Dream.

CHAPTER 9

LEVI

About the time I converted my auto mechanic and body shop into auto bays, we got some unexpected news from Israel. My cousin Yoni told me that his brother, Levi, had been released from prison in Israel and was following the rest of the family to Los Angeles. How he ended up in prison more than ten years earlier is quite a story.

Levi is ten years older than me. He was born in 1949, not long after Israel became a country. I was closer to Yoni, who is my age, but Levi and I had a lot in common. He was hyper and a go-getter, just like me, but he wasn't organized, and he never thought things through to their conclusion. And at a young age, he picked the wrong way of life.

We came from the same extended family, and we were always together, so we knew each other well. Levi's mother was my mother's sister, and their family lived only a couple of blocks away from us in Tel Aviv. Between the two families, there were about ten very close cousins, of whom Yoni and I were the youngest. Levi is closest in age to my older brothers, Jacob and Abe, and they formed a strong bond.

Even though I was significantly younger, Levi looked up to me. However, at the same time, he constantly tried to get me to join his less-than-legal lifestyle. I think he wanted me to run his petty criminal enterprises, but I never liked the idea of it and never got involved. I knew from an early age that what he was doing wasn't right—but he was family, and we had a good relationship with each other.

Our family was never privy to the details of Levi's crimes or attempted crimes, but it seemed like Levi was mostly doing minor burglaries, stealing electronics and other items that were easy to sell. These were small-time thefts, and I wouldn't have been surprised if the police had visited Levi's house a few times to ask him about the latest burglaries.

What Levi really wanted to do was prove that he was the biggest and the best, so he came up with an audacious theft that traumatized and scandalized Israel.

* * *

In the first decades of Israel's existence, there was almost no crime. There were very few murders, and armed robbery was virtually unheard of. Israel was a peaceful place and the people who lived there felt safe, apart from the occasional threats from outside forces that wanted to eliminate the nation altogether.

One of the reasons crime was so low was that it was difficult to get a gun in Israel. Other than the military and police, almost nobody had a gun back then—and if you had one, you were responsible for it. If you lost it, you were in trouble. If you sold it, you'd go to prison. One of our neighbors was in the army, so he had a gun like an Uzi submachine gun. He claimed he'd lost it, but in reality he probably sold it on the black market for $500 or $1,000, and he ended up being sent to prison for two years. Even today, the rate of gun ownership in Israel is low—fewer than 8 guns per 100 people, compared to more than 120 guns per 100 people in the US.

Nobody in Israel expected crime to happen, especially crimes involving guns, which is why it was so shocking when Levi and a small gang of his friends pulled hoods over their heads to hide their faces and walked into one of the biggest banks in the city of Ashdod while brandishing Uzis.

Bank robbery was something we saw in Hollywood movies, but nobody thought it could happen in Israel—and nobody had ever heard of ordinary citizens like Levi walking around with illegal Uzis.

Israeli banks didn't have much in the way of security other than a sleepy guard and a standard alarm. Even so, I think Levi chose the bank in Ashdod—which is south of Tel Aviv on the Mediterranean Sea—rather than one in Tel Aviv because it was less likely to have a sophisticated security system. As it turned out, it was pretty easy for Levi and his gang to get the bank staff to stuff as much cash as possible into their bags while the terrified customers looked on in horror.

However, before Levi and his gang left, a bank teller managed to set off the alarm, which was so loud that everyone on the street knew there was a problem. A bus driver heard the alarm and when he looked up, he saw the robbers run out of the bank with bags full of cash and jump into the getaway car. The bank was on a narrow road with a busy market, so there was only one way out—and the driver pulled his bus across the street to block the exit.

In their desperation, a couple of the robbers—including Levi—jumped out of the car and shot at the bus while screaming for the driver to move. Nobody was hit, but the driver moved the bus and Levi's gang got away with what today would be hundreds of thousands of dollars.

* * *

Levi disappeared for a while after the robbery, but at the time nobody knew why. The robbery was headline news, and even though I was only eleven, I understood that it was a major event. It was one of the first armed bank robberies in Israel's history, and it was certainly the biggest and most spectacular. Suddenly, people were more suspicious of strangers—but we still had no idea that Levi was involved.

About this time, I remember hearing the former Israeli prime minister talking on TV about crime. I'm not sure if he was discussing this particular bank robbery, but the point he was making was that Israel couldn't be a real country without crime. Bank robberies and other crimes proved that Israel was a legitimate nation, because it's impossible to create a place with no crime. It was an interesting viewpoint, and perhaps he was trying to appease people's fears now that armed bank robbery was a reality in the country.

One of Levi's fellow robbers was about eighteen or nineteen, and he was the first to be connected to the robbery and arrested. It was his car that was used for the getaway, and they traced the car to him. He made a plea deal with the police, naming the other robbers in exchange for a lighter sentence. One of those he named was Levi, but the way the police definitively connected Levi to the robbery was bizarre.

In the trunk of the car was a blanket with dog hair on it, and when the police went to Levi's home to interview him, they saw his dog—a collie like Lassie, who was probably the most beloved dog in Israel—and matched the dog's hair to the dog hair on the blanket. Because of that and the word of the younger thief, the police had no trouble putting Levi at the scene of the crime.

Our whole family was stunned to find out that Levi had been arrested for the heist. He had never been a saint and was often on the verge of being in trouble with the police, but nobody imagined he was capable of helping to pull off what was the biggest armed robbery in the history of Israel to that date. Even my brothers, who were among Levi's closest friends, never knew he was involved until the day he was arrested.

There was a huge trial and Levi's mother—my aunt— spent a lot of money on lawyers to defend him. My uncle wasn't so generous, and he basically wanted nothing to do with his son. He was very disappointed, and I'm sure he wasn't as surprised as the rest of us when Levi was arrested.

Levi was found guilty of the bank robbery and sentenced to a lengthy time in prison. He actually received extra time because he was the one who had shot the Uzi at the bus, and people could have been killed. Levi went to prison in 1971, two years before I left for Los Angeles. I had never forgotten about Levi, but I assumed he'd be in an Israeli prison forever and that I'd never see him again.

That's why it was such a surprise when Yoni told me that Levi had been released from prison after slightly more than ten years and was planning to come to Los Angeles. My whole extended family was thrilled at the thought of seeing him, and they planned a huge party to welcome him. His mother spent every waking moment arranging his welcome party.

*   *   *

Out of all the people in Levi's world, his own father was possibly the one person who knew my cousin was capable of terrible things. About a year before the bank robbery, the way Levi's father felt about him became quite clear to me.

My grandfather threw a huge party at his house, which was only a couple of blocks from our house in Tel Aviv. I was excited to be there with Yoni and lots of other cousins and friends. We were hanging around as kids do, making a lot of noise, but one of the neighbors didn't like the commotion. He'd seen me plenty of times at my grandfather's, and he knew that I collected pigeons. He came up to me and said, "Look, you kids are making a lot of noise. If you keep it quiet, I'll give you a pair of doves."

Of course, I immediately agreed. The neighbor was also a collector of pigeons, and I'd seen his birds before. He had lovely pigeons and doves, including some very unusual and expensive ones. I was excited about the deal, so I made sure the kids kept the noise down, especially when they were near this neighbor's house.

When the party ended late that evening, Yoni and I went over to the neighbor's house and knocked on his door. When he answered, I asked for the birds he'd promised me. He looked at me and yelled, "Get the hell out of here before I give you five across the face!"

"But you promised me the pigeons for keeping the kids quiet," I said.

"You should have kept quiet anyway," he said and slammed the door in my face.

I felt like I was entitled to those pigeons because that was his side of the deal, so I told Yoni that we weren't leaving without the pigeons I'd been promised. We waited until the neighbor went to bed and I was certain he'd fallen asleep, then we went to the back of his house and stole a pair of pigeons from the cages. They were standard pigeons—not any of his special or rare birds. When I got home, I put them in one of the cages on the roof of my house.

The next day, the neighbor showed up at our house while I was at school and made a big fuss about the missing pigeons. He also went to Yoni's house and did the same thing.

That afternoon when I was walking back from school, my sister Mijil ran up to me. "Oh, you're in big trouble," she told me. "Mom and Pop are looking for you. They're pissed off because you stole the neighbor's pigeons."

She also told me that Yoni was being beaten by his father at that very moment because the neighbor had accused the two of us of stealing the pigeons together. So I ran home, got on my bike, and raced over to Yoni's house. As I arrived there, I heard him yelling at his father, who was beating him with his belt, "It wasn't me! It wasn't me!"

"I don't need another Levi!" his father yelled back. "There's already one Levi in this family. I don't need another one."

That's when I knew my uncle was suffering under the stress of Levi's evil streak, and that he was trying to stop Yoni from going down the same path—so I rushed home and released the pigeons. I knew that once they were free, they would find their way back to their original cages. Right after I let them go, my parents came outside and asked me if I'd stolen the pigeons from the neighbor. Unlike Yoni, I was lucky enough that my parents always trusted me. I asked them to check the neighbor's cages to see if the birds were really missing. When they went over there, the pigeons were back in their cages and the guy had to admit he'd made a mistake.

That episode taught me some important lessons. First,

even though you might feel you are entitled to something, you cannot just go in there and take it without permission, because that is stealing. Luckily, I was able to make my own situation right, albeit at the expense of Yoni's backside. Second, Yoni was not only a close cousin but a good friend. He claimed only that it wasn't him. He was with me, so he knew it was me, but he never ratted me out. And third, it's important not to jump to conclusions. Yoni's father panicked and beat him before knowing all the facts, whereas my parents verified my story. Fortunately, they didn't know the *full* story, and by the time they checked it out, everything was back to normal.

*   *   *

Everyone was hopeful that Levi would settle down and make a fresh start in Los Angeles, but it didn't take long for him to drift back into his old ways. No matter where he went, he seemed to have no trouble finding shady connections. He also claimed to know who had shot Micky Levine in Tel Aviv—and without saying it, he made it seem like I owed him a favor. That scared me.

When Levi showed up one day with Vince, one of Micky's thugs, I got freaked out even more. He tried to convince me that there was easy money in a robbery he was planning. I told him I wasn't interested. I was making good money from honest hard work, and I could see a future with Aline. Getting into a life of crime was the last thing on my mind. I told him not just *no* but *hell no*. Once again, I could see a fork in the road—go with Levi and regret everything, or do my own thing and be proud of my life.

Pretty soon, Levi was stealing jewelry from rich show-offs. He knew the United States was the land of opportunity, but what he underestimated was how much opportunity there was for his particular line of work. That's when he decided to expand into the drug business, essentially taking over the void left by Micky, and he once again tried to bully me into joining him. Just like before, I let him know I wouldn't do it. "It's not who I am," I told him. It was certainly who he was, though.

After that, I didn't see much of Levi, but I heard the stories and rumors. He was still chasing the almighty dollar, but his new lifestyle had shifted from being a secretive "Most Wanted," high-end burglar to becoming a distributor of Colombian cocaine. His new boss was Hector, the king of the cocaine trade. As his star in the subculture of organized crime began to rise, Levi moved into a Beverly Hills mansion and thought he was living the American Dream.

Meanwhile, Vince was working for Levi, and they got into an argument after a shipment came up short. Vince, who was more than likely guilty, panicked at being discovered and pulled a gun, shooting Levi twice. But Levi was lucky. The bullets passed through without hitting anything vital. Vince was not so lucky. A few days later, he ended up in a dumpster with a bullet in his head. Apparently, the way to stay alive in that world was to finish what you started.

Getting shot changed Levi in a big way. He wanted to get

out of the drug trade and decided to make a fresh start back home in Israel. With millions of hidden dollars, he had enough money to retire and be happy for the rest of life, and he set his plan in motion. He bought an impressive mansion outside Tel Aviv and began shipping containers filled with furnishings— and probably cash—from Los Angeles.

At the same time, the Drug Enforcement Administration discovered a huge shipment of Hector's cocaine. Despite his shortcomings, Levi wasn't dumb enough to leave a paper trail, so it was never connected to him. However, there was speculation among the drug dealers that to hasten his exit and create a diversion, Levi may have tipped off the DEA. When newspapers reported on the amount of cocaine seized, it fell far short of the amount Hector expected. The missing cocaine had a street value of $2.8 million, and the Colombians were blaming Levi and accusing him of stealing it.

Not long after this discovery, and just as he was preparing to leave for the airport for his flight to Israel, Levi was ambushed and shot to death on the street outside Yoni's home. There was no doubt about who did it or why. True to form, Levi didn't finish what he started. In his rush to get out, he left too many loose ends untied and didn't think his plan through to its conclusion.

But that solved only half of the Colombians' problem. They still didn't have the missing cocaine or the $2.8 million they claimed Levi had stolen from them. About a week later, Yoni did not come home one night. His wife, Amy, started to worry and tried to call him on his cell phone, but there was no

109

answer. About midnight, she got a distressing phone call from the Colombians, telling her they'd kidnapped her husband. They warned her that the only way to see Yoni alive again was to deliver the money to them. If they didn't get the money, or if she called the police, they would kill Yoni. There were no options, so she called me and my brother Jacob in tears, asking us for help.

Jacob and I were petrified, not just for Yoni but for our own families—but it was up to us to figure it out. The Colombians gave us twenty-four hours to give them what they wanted, but nobody had any idea if the money even existed or where it was if it did. It was like being in a movie, but I was living it in real time and the clock was ticking. We were warned not to call the police, so I got together with Amy and Jacob to think of something.

A few days before he was killed, Levi visited Yoni and left some boxes at his house. He told Yoni that he was going to have the boxes shipped to Israel once he got there. We thought there might be something of value in them, so the three of us spent the night going through the boxes until we found a receipt for a storage unit in New Jersey. The note attached to the receipt listed the things that Levi was storing in the unit and was planning to send on to Israel later—including a word in Hebrew: *mezuman*. Cash!

It was all we had to go on, so Jacob and I caught the next flight to New York. To make a long story short, we found the storage unit and the cash hidden in a TV box, and we returned the cash to the Colombians. They released Yoni, and that's the last we ever heard from them. We'd made a deal with the devil, but we were free of Levi's underworld life.

The end result was that we saved Yoni. Some people may see it as the bad guys winning because they got the illegal drug money back, but these were the same people who had killed Levi, and I have no doubt that they would have killed Yoni as well. So, yes, they won in one respect because they got the money back, but we also won because we got Yoni back—and in my opinion, our victory was greater.

Unfortunately, this sort of thing happens all the time and people have to make decisions based on what seems right at the time. For example, soldiers frequently get kidnapped by terrorist organizations, and their government exchanges one— or even dozens or hundreds—of prisoners for that soldier, even though they know the prisoners are guilty of terrorism and may come back and kill again. It's a fact of diplomatic life, and what we did to get Yoni back was no different.

* * *

At the time he was killed, Levi was very wealthy. We had no idea how much money he had, but we found out later that he was worth many millions. He bought a gorgeous mansion in Beverly Hills with drug money. He bought a spectacular mansion in Tel Aviv with drug money. He bought several Mercedes and shipped them to Israel. He bought the most beautiful Mercedes in Los Angeles. All with drug money. He was living the lifestyle you'd see in *Miami Vice*. But in the end, he was killed on the street at the age of forty, shortly before moving back to Israel. Every dime he made from the drug trade was lost. Everything was wasted.

Despite all that she knew, including the source of his money, Levi's mother never lost faith in him. She loved her boy passionately, perhaps as only a mother can. His death might have been predictable, but she was still devastated by it—and she wanted something good to come from it.

The only money of Levi's that she took was $1 million to build a synagogue in Tel Aviv. She named it the House of Levi, and it is the only thing that survived from all the millions of dollars that Levi accumulated and wasted. It is heartening to know that the House of Levi is still doing good work and is beneficial to the community.

People often ask me if I knew what Levi was like—and if I did, why I didn't turn him in to the police or the FBI. We were cousins, but shortly after he arrived in Los Angeles our paths seldom crossed; he went his own way and I went mine, and we drifted apart. I knew he wasn't an angel, but I never knew what was actually going on. All I heard were vague rumors from other family members, and I don't think any of them knew the truth either.

In Levi's case, what he was doing was wrong, and I didn't like it (especially after he tried to coerce me into joining his gang), so I disengaged myself from his life. I only heard things about him from other family members, but I chose to look the other way and didn't think I should be the one to turn him in based on mere rumors and speculation. Instead of focusing my energy on Levi, I used his example as the opposite of what I wanted for my own life as I built my business and family in a legitimate way.

For me and the rest of the family, Levi's death was another reminder that nothing good comes from bad decisions. Levi wanted the good life, but he was always trying to find the shortcut. It may have worked for a moment, but it was never going to work in the long run. I resolved to continue along the path I had carved out for myself, a path that let me live a beautiful life with a clear conscience.

CHAPTER 10

TRACT HOMES

Throughout my life, I have been inspired by my older brothers, Jacob and Abe. Like me, they had a passion for cars, but at about the same time I was building my auto bays, they demolished their auto shop and built what turned out to be a successful shopping center on the site. Now we were all landlords, and I started wondering how I could follow in their footsteps and even take my business a few steps further.

Meanwhile, my auto bays were doing well, and they took care of themselves for several years. I built four sets of auto bays—three on Pico Boulevard and one on Venice Boulevard— and I collected the rents every month. This gave me the freedom to enjoy my life with Aline and start my family with the birth of my first son, Eric, in 1984.

All along, I kept thinking about how I could expand my businesses, even if it meant doing something new. As I drove around Los Angeles in the 1980s, I noticed developers turning open, vacant land into attractive homes, and I realized that I could do this as well as anyone else—even though I'd never built a house before. All I needed was the inspiration and a little help from the banks.

In 1986, I came across a vacant lot in the San Fernando Valley, and I bought it with the idea of building homes on it. It was about two acres of land in a residential area, and I checked the zoning and did all my due diligence. I found out that I could subdivide the land, so I divided it into eight decent-sized lots with the idea of building a single-family home on each lot.

The San Fernando Valley lies to the north and northwest of downtown Los Angeles. It became part of LA in the early twentieth century, and today it makes up a major section of the Los Angeles metropolitan area. It includes cities such as Burbank, Van Nuys, Panorama City, Sherman Oaks, and Northridge, as well as Warner Bros. Studios, Walt Disney Studios, and Universal Studios Hollywood. It is a popular place to live because it is not as expensive as some other areas such as Beverly Hills, Brentwood, Santa Monica, and West Hollywood, but it is convenient to downtown and has easy access to most of Greater Los Angeles thanks to the major highways that pass through it.

Buying a two-acre lot in the San Fernando Valley made sense from a business standpoint. The Valley (as it is known) was growing fast, and people needed homes. I paid about $600,000 for the land, and once it was subdivided, each of the eight lots had values between $60,000 to $85,000, depending on their size. At that time, the average price in LA to build the type of house I envisioned was between $150,000 to $175,000, again depending on the size and whether it came with a pool. I had plans drawn up, pulled all the necessary permits, and went to work building eight houses.

All in all, each house cost me about $200,000 to $225,000, including the land. The houses—which I built all at the same time to take advantage of economies of scale—were about 2,500–3,000 square feet with three bedrooms, three bathrooms, two-car garages, and nice backyards. Some even had pools in the backyard. These were really nice houses that people wanted to buy, and I sold them for $300,000 to $350,000 each, which left me with a profit of about $100,000 on each home—or roughly $800,000 for all eight homes.

One of the main reasons that building these homes was a success was that I maintained control over everything. I owned the land, drafted the building plans, and put those plans into action. Only when the houses were finished did I hand everything over to a broker to sell.

When I look back on that moment in the late 1980s and realize the journey I had taken from running my first burger joints to pocketing an $800,000 profit on a single venture, I appreciate how fortunate I have been and how the gods were smiling on me through the years. So much could have gone wrong, but by carefully planning and not allowing myself to get greedy, I was able to reap the rewards and move on to other projects.

* * *

The type of construction I was getting involved in is known as "tract housing"—because the houses are built on larger tracts of land that are subdivided into smaller lots.

The concept of tract housing developed after World War II when millions of American veterans returned home from service overseas and took advantage of the G.I. Bill that helped them transition from soldiers to civilians. One of the key parts of the bill was a provision that gave the veterans low-interest loans with no money down for a home or business. This led to a postwar housing boom, mostly among first-time home buyers, and the most economical way to provide the much-needed housing was to build great numbers of almost-identical houses on a large piece of land that had been subdivided into smaller parcels.

This building method provided good, inexpensive housing, mostly near or in existing cities. Many of the areas were just outside the cities, leading to the expansion of suburbs, complete with schools, churches, shopping areas, and all the infrastructure necessary to encourage a thriving community.

Among the first—and by far the most famous—tract home developments was Levittown, about thirty miles east of New York City on Long Island, New York. The town was a planned community for veterans of World War II, and work on the first two thousand homes started in 1947. By 1951, Levittown had expanded to more than seventeen thousand new homes over several square miles, allowing thousands of families to become homeowners instead of renters.

Building new homes was a boon to the economy. Vast numbers of people were employed to build the homes, and it gave millions of families a step up to home ownership and an easy entry into middle-class life. It also coincided with the baby boom, and millions of kids across the US grew up in these homes.

However, tract homes weren't always popular. They were often criticized because so many were built in areas that were outside the cities and, as a result, made homeowners reliant on automobiles. At the same time, the attraction of the suburbs helped lead to the decline of downtown areas across America. Pete Seeger's 1963 hit song "Little Boxes" was an indictment against tract housing and urban sprawl, referring to the houses as poorly built "little boxes" that "all look just the same."

While it was true that some housing was built cheaply, giving the whole concept of tract homes a bad reputation, building these homes was no different from building a single home on a single lot. The ones I built, and most of the others I saw in Los Angeles in the 1980s, were well-constructed, solid houses that have withstood the test of time. Every tract home I built is still standing and has significantly increased in value. In fact, the very first tract houses I built are now worth as much as $1 million each.

Over time, the success of Levittown inspired other developments in New York and beyond. Most were much smaller, but they followed the same general idea: build as many new houses as possible on a plot of land, while still offering decent-sized yards and amenities such as pools and garages.

I was very familiar with the San Fernando Valley, which is where I built my first homes. It was where my brothers had rented an apartment when they arrived in Los Angeles in 1973 and where I first went to school when I joined them. Interestingly, some of the largest real estate developers in the Valley were Jewish, and at a time when anti-Semitism was still rampant, they broke the barriers to home ownership in the 1950s and 1960s. Among the most famous developers were Lawrence Weinberg, who built thousands of homes in the Valley, and Nathan Shapell, who also branched out into high-rise buildings in downtown Los Angeles.

By the time I started building homes in the Valley, Eli Broad and Donald Kaufman—who founded the company that became KB Home—were already heavily invested in tract homes in the Valley.

* * *

As soon as my first eight houses were finished, I started looking for another project. I had proven to the banks and to the other builders in Los Angeles that I was serious and that I could turn an idea into a success, and I let the real estate brokers know what I was looking for. I went on to build many more homes across Los Angeles.

Tract Homes

Today it's almost impossible to find an open piece of land anywhere in Greater Los Angeles, but it was still possible in the late 1980s and early 1990s. More importantly, it was still affordable for someone like me who had bigger plans in mind. Nonetheless, there were added obstacles to consider when buying land, such as hills—which can lead to landslides—and the proximity of things such as schools, roads, and places to shop.

The types of homes I was trying to build were the ones that the average homebuyer in Los Angeles in the late 1980s and early 1990s could afford. I wasn't trying to get into the luxury homes that would appeal to wealthy clients such as movie stars and professional athletes. The sector I was after was people who wanted well-built homes with about 2,500 to 3,000 square feet of living area that were priced around $250,000 to $350,000. I wanted to keep the homes affordable and therefore attractive to a large segment of the population. Although $250,000 to $350,000 may seem high for that era and was more than double the national average, it was more or less in line with the average home price in Los Angeles in the early 1990s.

My brother Jacob, inspired by the success of his shopping mall and of my homes, also started building houses. His idea was to build custom homes for wealthy clients, which could easily run into the millions of dollars. I didn't want to get into that market at that point in my career because it was risky—and I've never been one to take unnecessary risks. The way I looked at it, with even a little change in the real estate market or a minor recession, the bottom could quickly drop out of the market for custom homes. Even in a recession, however, people still need homes and there will always be a market for average-priced homes.

I built about two hundred single-family homes by the mid-1990s. I always made sure the architecture was consistent with the neighborhood, whether it was Spanish-style or traditional townhomes or anything in between. Also, I wanted each house to be a little different, so I never went with the "little boxes" cookie-cutter approach. At the very minimum, I changed the facades and the locations of the garage.

I enjoyed this line of work, and whenever I saw an opportunity, I took it. In the mid-1990s, I bought a couple hundred apartments in the Mid-Wilshire neighborhood of Los Angeles. The building was run by a slumlord and was in terrible shape, but I renovated the units and helped transform the neighborhood. It became a comfortable place for families from all walks of life to live.

At the same time, I bought a hundred-unit building in the San Fernando Valley that had also seen better days. These were very big units with great potential. I renovated the entire property, converting the apartments into condominiums and adding a lot of amenities such as pools, a spa, and a gym. The difference between an apartment and a condominium is that apartments are rental units, whereas condominiums allow people to purchase the units and become homeowners.

I have always been an advocate of home ownership, so

my team of brokers reached out to the existing tenants and explained to them that they would be better off owning their own units than being renters. With the help of first-time homebuyer programs, they were able to buy the units with a down payment as low as 3 percent and at an attractive interest rate. Most of the tenants had never owned property before and were surprised to learn that at the end of the day, the mortgage, homeowner association fees, property taxes, and other fees combined were less than the rent they were paying. Most of them seized the opportunity to buy, and the project was a huge success. We helped about one hundred renters become new homeowners.

I've always been conservative with finances, and I followed the same winning strategy that I used when I expanded my auto bays: never fall into the trap of becoming overleveraged. From my experience, that is the first rule of business. When you're not overleveraged, you can give yourself a buffer so you can survive if anything goes wrong. I think it's because of this philosophy that I've never lost money on a project.

Not being overleveraged stems from the advice given to me by Alan Riseman in 1978, when I bought the old gas station that became my first auto shop: "Every opportunity you have to buy, buy it."

In any business, you take nothing for granted, and I always knew that even if the market turned and I was forced to sell my houses for less than I wanted, I could still break even. If I was breaking even, I was still in the game.

The key thing I did with any new piece of property was to make sure the loan was sensible for the project I had in mind. This may sound obvious, but I have seen too many otherwise brilliant and intelligent developers lose their businesses because they took too many risks. They literally lost everything. The only difference between me and them was that I was more conservative. They often became overleveraged, leaving them in the hole and scrambling to avoid bankruptcy.

For homes in my price range, there was no need to put in high-end kitchens and high-end bathrooms—but everything was still top quality, and it was appropriate for that type of house. Once you start adding the high-end features, you're taking a risk by making the house too expensive. I'd seen other builders do exactly that—for example, building a $300,000 house but adding all sorts of fancy features and putting it on the market for $425,000. Buyers know when a house is overpriced, which often leads to these properties failing to sell. In cases like this, the builders inevitably got burned and had to take a loss to get rid of the properties.

Losing it all may be the chance you take when you buy a piece of land and build several houses on it, but the stakes become higher as the number of houses increases. When you build seventy or eighty homes all at once, everything gets multiplied, including the risk. It's much harder to finance even a small portion of such large developments with your own money, so it becomes almost inevitable that you'll be overdependent on the banks. I've seen the ugly consequences of shifting markets and events beyond anyone's control, and it's not something I ever want to be part of.

I'm also a very lucky guy. I have never been in a "worst-case scenario," and I have always managed to make a profit on my projects. I made a profit on every one of the two hundred or so single-family homes I built—and later, when I got into converting historical buildings into thousands of apartments and residential lofts, I made a profit on those as well.

I have also learned that instinct is very important when it comes to property development. When you see an empty piece of land or an existing building, you usually get a feeling one way or the other—you think it's a good prospect and you can see what the possibilities are . . . or it seems like a loser. There's no way to teach anyone how to trust their instincts. For me, they have developed with experience.

Another essential part of my business success is that I've never pretended that I know everything or that I can do everything. When I opened my burger joints, I couldn't cook the burgers and fries, so I hired the best cooks I could find because they knew how to do it. In the auto shops, I didn't know how to build an engine or knock a dent out of a fender, so I hired the best mechanics and bodyworkers around. What I am good at is finding the right people to help me meet my goals, and the same thing applies in the real estate business.

I can swing a hammer, replace a burned-out light bulb, and even design a house, but I can't physically build a house, pour concrete, or run an electrical wire through a wall. I'm smart enough to know that, and I'm smart enough to hire the right people who specialize in those skills. I'm just an average guy who dropped out of high school. But I've learned some important lessons—how to work with people and how to bring my own visions to life.

Even when I eventually started building luxury homes in the multimillion-dollar range, I still followed this same strategy. If it worked for tract homes, I figured it would also work for other types of homes, and I was correct.

*   *   *

Of all the single-family homes I have built over the years, the house I am most proud of is the one I built for myself in 2000. I bought a small house on a big piece of land in Beverly Hills, but I demolished the house and built a bigger home where my children grew up. Even though it was for my own family and was where I saw myself living for the rest of my life, I still didn't take any chances. I followed the same rules that I applied to any other building project, making sure I was living within my means and not taking any unnecessary risks.

Another valuable piece of advice I have followed through the years is that you can't get stuck on just one way of doing things. That's why I was able to move from burger joints to auto shops and then to building tract homes and ultimately mansions worth tens of millions of dollars.

TRACT HOMES

After I'd built about two hundred homes in the Greater Los Angeles area, I came to another fork in the road, and I recognized the opportunity to expand once again—this time in downtown Los Angeles and into a completely different type of building.

CHAPTER 11

HIGH-RISE

O ne day in early 1991, when I'd finished one of my tract-home developments and was looking for my next project, I got a phone call from my brother Jacob. Like me, Jacob had moved into the real estate business several years earlier. Our businesses were completely separate with different plans and objectives, and other than family matters, we kept out of each other's way. I count myself as being very lucky when it came to making the right decisions and never losing money, but Jacob often took on riskier projects and sometimes he had setbacks.

When he called me that day in 1991, Jacob told me that he'd made an offer and put down a deposit on an empty high-rise building in historic downtown Los Angeles. He had agreed to buy the building from Union Bank for $1.3 million. The previous owner had lost it to the bank when all the tenants left and he could no longer make the payments. It's the same thing as banks foreclosing on a home when a homeowner stops paying the mortgage. Unfortunately, the timing proved to be terrible for Jacob because he'd just had a setback on another project and wasn't going to be able to fulfill his commitment—but he didn't want to walk away. He believed it was a great building and that it offered an excellent opportunity for development.

Jacob knew I had just made a good profit on my latest homes, and he asked me to come and look at the property with him to see if it would be something I would be interested in. The high-rise was a beautiful, historic, fourteen-story office building at 639 South Spring Street in the heart of the historic downtown Los Angeles area. Spring Street was once a bustling street in a busy downtown. It was the center of the old financial district, and 639 South Spring Street was originally built in 1925 as the Los Angeles Stock Exchange building. It was now an empty shell on a depressed street, but it still looked very impressive to me.

Jacob suggested that I could partner with him to purchase the building. He really wanted to make the deal happen, but he just was not able to do it on his own at the time. Owning a high-rise was something that had always been appealing to me. It signaled "success" in a dramatic way, and my heart told me I'd never regret it. I was thirty-one years old, and it was very tempting to step in and make the high-rise at 639 South Spring Street the exclamation mark on my career.

The price Jacob was negotiating seemed low for the potential of the building—that is, if it had been located somewhere else. The problem was that there was limited opportunity because of building regulations at that time in downtown Los Angeles. It was a historic building, so it essentially had to keep its traditional purpose. It was possible to purchase the building, but renovating it would come with millions of restrictions. When *adaptive reuse* came along—the process of repurposing a building from its original use to a new and different use—it eased many of those restrictions.

I didn't know much about this type of building, but I quickly realized that $1.3 million was too much in its present state as a vacant property and with the current building regulations in place. I suggested to Jacob that it was overpriced, so he and I went to Union Bank and renegotiated the terms that Jacob had agreed to. We made a joint offer of $850,000 to take the building off their hands—a significant reduction from the original $1.3 million. Jacob thought it was crazy to make such a lowball offer, but I knew the building was a burden to the bank and they didn't want to be stuck with it. Besides, there were no other interested buyers. We had nothing to lose.

I explained everything to the bank officials and made my offer, and it surprised even me that they accepted it in place of Jacob's earlier agreement. So Jacob and I ended up buying 639 South Spring Street for $850,000. In reality, it cost a lot more; there was no income from tenants and we still had to pay property taxes, maintenance, and cleaning costs. Holding on to an empty building costs money, especially a building of that size— about 130,000 square feet.

There was no logical reason to buy the building, at least not while the city of Los Angeles made it impossible to do anything useful with it and not until the area had been revitalized. This was why the previous owner had decided to sell, but I bought it for the prestige and because it was a beautiful building. At the age of thirty-one, I finally had my high-rise.

After a while, Jacob came to me and explained that he'd had some problems with other projects and couldn't afford the expenses for the high-rise. He wanted out, but I told him that if we sold it, we'd have to do so at a discount—and that I really didn't want to sell at a discount because I saw the potential for the future. We'd already seen that other developers had no interest in it. Taking everything into consideration, I was willing to hang on to the building and lose money in the short term, because I believed my investment would pay off later. Jacob, however, didn't have that luxury, and he couldn't afford to wait.

When I told Jacob that I didn't want to sell, he asked me to help him out by buying his share of the building. I told him I wasn't going to take advantage of him, so I couldn't do that. I knew the building offered opportunity in the years ahead, and I told Jacob I didn't want him to look back later and resent that I'd bought him out when he was in distress. Instead, I told him that I would cover all the costs for a while, until he got things sorted out.

Not long after we came to that agreement, Jacob came back to me and told me he didn't want me to carry the financial burden any longer and he had to sell right away because he needed the cash. Again, I didn't want to benefit from my brother's misfortune, so I asked a good friend, Danny, if he was interested in joining me. I had done other projects with Danny over the years, so he knew he could trust me on a deal like this. He agreed to buy Jacob's share at a discount.

Fast-forward to a couple of years later, and nothing much had changed. The building was still vacant, the area was still somewhat run-down, and we were still spending a lot of money on taxes and maintenance. Danny was growing impatient, and he wanted to sell. I encouraged him to hold on, explaining that there was talk of new regulations that would allow owners like us to adapt our buildings for new uses. There was huge potential, but Danny had come to the end of the line and was not willing to put any more money into the project. "It's a bottomless pit," he told me.

I ended up buying Danny's share, paying him a couple hundred thousand dollars more than he'd paid Jacob. He was happy to be out of the project, and I was now the sole owner of the high-rise at 639 South Spring Street. Less than a year later, the Los Angeles City Council passed the Adaptive Reuse Ordinance that I had been hoping for. After eight years of sitting on an empty high-rise building, I was finally able to do something with it.

* * *

The high-rise at 639 South Spring Street was only a few blocks north of where I opened my first burger joint in 1975, so I knew the area well. The 600 block of South Spring Street is in the center of what is known as the Historic Core of downtown

Los Angeles. It was previously known as the Financial District, and it was built up as the downtown area between the turn of the twentieth century and the 1930s. It is full of elegant and charming old multistory buildings that were originally department stores, offices, and the greatest movie palaces in the world.

The movie palaces were concentrated along Broadway— one block to the west of South Spring Street—and were built at the height of the Hollywood movie industry in the 1920s and 1930s. There were twelve movie theaters in a six-block section of Broadway, which was more than in any other similar area in the world. Some of the theaters had more than two thousand seats, and together the twelve movie theaters had more than fifteen thousand seats.

If you lived in Los Angeles in the 1920s and 1930s, this was the place where glitzy premieres were attended and where thousands of moviegoers flocked to every night of the week. Most of the facades still stand, and all but a few have been refurbished. Before the COVID-19 pandemic began in 2020, many of these theaters were still used for live shows and entertainment. Looking at them, it's easy to imagine what it was like in the 1930s to walk down the street and be overwhelmed by the neon lights and the throngs of people.

Broadway was also the main commercial street and one of the oldest streets in the city, dating back to 1849 when it was known as Fort Street. By the mid-twentieth century, there were several major department stores on Broadway. Day and night, it was a busy and colorful thoroughfare, teeming with shoppers and moviegoers—and the excitement extended to South Spring Street, which had its share of hotels, stores, and banks. When the spectacular Los Angeles Stock Exchange Building was built across the street from 639 South Spring Street, my building had been adapted to offices and other uses.

The Historic Core remained the central business district of Los Angeles until the 1950s, when the suburbs started attracting more people and it was no longer necessary to go downtown to shop or go to the movies. People still came downtown, but not like they used to. Many theaters and department stores closed and banks moved, ushering in a period of decline that coincided with the national trend of downtowns being abandoned in favor of the suburbs. Some of the banks were used as movie locations—in fact, the bank robbery scene in my own movie, *For the Love of Money*, was shot in one of these old abandoned banks. (I'll talk about my movie in later chapters.)

By the time I arrived in LA in 1973, the area was known more for its street gang problem than as a desirable destination. Also at this time, the new downtown area known as Bunker Hill was being developed just north of the Historic Core. Fifty-, sixty-, and seventy-story skyscrapers were being built here, and I remember watching many of these giants going up when I drove to my burger joints. When these skyscrapers opened, the last occupants of office buildings like mine at 639 South Spring Street moved a few blocks to Bunker Hill and into new, modern facilities.

Even though that part of downtown Los Angeles wasn't

doing so well in 1991 and there was very little development going on in the neighborhood, I knew that better days lay ahead. As I walked around and looked at these beautiful buildings, it was obvious to me that they would someday come back to life. I knew I only had to wait, and I was fortunate enough to have the good luck and the money to do just that.

* * *

When Jacob and I bought 639 South Spring Street in 1991, we had to figure out what to do with it while we waited for the city to change the regulations. The building was completely vacant, and it was impossible to find tenants. Other than the appeal of new and modern office space in a prestigious skyscraper or in a booming suburb, one of the major problems with my high-rise was that it was not air-conditioned. By the 1990s, air-conditioning had become essential, even in the mild Los Angeles climate. Businesses could get everything they wanted, including air-conditioning, just a few blocks away in Bunker Hill or farther afield in the suburbs.

That didn't mean our high-rise remained unused. I was paying property taxes on the building and paying for the maintenance to keep it in good shape. There were no tenants, but I managed to generate income by renting the building out for movie and television show locations as well as for commercials and music videos. Fortunately, Los Angeles was—and still is—the center of the entertainment world, and there was always a demand for locations—and the advantage of an empty building is that production companies can make it into anything they want. The building became known as a great location for filming, so this helped me cover some of my costs. At least I wasn't losing too much money by sitting on an empty building.

One of the first movies that used my high-rise was *Wolf* with Jack Nicholson, which was released in 1994. Other famous movies include *Fatal Attraction* (1987) with Michael Douglas and Glenn Close, *The Wedding Singer* (1998) with Adam Sandler, *Spider-Man* (2002), *Transformers* (2007), *Inception* (2010), *Think like a Man* (2012), and *Being the Ricardos* (2021).

I've always loved movies, so to me it was a thrill to lease my space out to production companies, and I'd often go down to the set to see how things were going. I met a lot of stars that way, including Jack Nicholson. I also learned the hard—and embarrassing—way that some stars don't look the same in real life as they do on the big screen.

One day I met a producer at the building to negotiate a two-week lease to shoot a movie there. We met for forty-five minutes to work out the details, and when we were finished and the producer left, the location scout turned to me and asked, "Do you know who you were negotiating with?" I said I never caught his name, so he told me, "That was Sean Penn."

"You've got to be kidding me!" I said. "I was negotiating with Sean Penn all this time and I never realized it?"

"I figured you didn't know who it was," he said. "Most people are excited to talk to someone who's won two Academy

Awards for Best Actor, but you talked to him just like he was an ordinary guy off the street."

My friends and family have never let me live this down, and they still ask me things like, "Would you know Sean Penn if you met him?" Apparently not. He did a great job of acting like a normal guy.

The list of television shows that were shot at my high-rise is even longer. Among them are *NCIS*, *NYPD Blue*, *Perry Mason*, *Grey's Anatomy*, *Project Runway,* and *Homeland*. Lots of music stars also made music videos at that location. If you check out the videos "Happy" by Pharrell Williams, "A Milli" by Lil Wayne, and "TKO" by Justin Timberlake, you'll see scenes that were shot in and around the building. Others who made music videos there include Ariana Grande, Eminem, Beyoncé, Nick Jonas, and Cardi B.

* * *

In 1999, the landscape changed in LA—literally. The city of Los Angeles passed the Adaptive Reuse Ordinance, which allows property owners like me to convert the upper floors of historic downtown buildings into work and living space lofts. After owning the high-rise at 639 South Spring Street for eight years, I finally saw the opportunity I had been hoping for—the chance to turn an empty historic building into something new while keeping the integrity of the building and the neighborhood.

Quite simply, Adaptive Reuse means that a building can

be used for a purpose other than the one for which it was built. In the case of 639 South Spring Street, the building was originally used for offices with some retail space on the street level, and until 1999 the zoning regulations did not allow any deviation from its intended purpose. Now I was free to make something out of the building. The rules are that 33 percent has to be living space and 67 percent has to be workspace.

Adaptive Reuse is the most logical and cost-effective way to revitalize the Historic Core of downtown Los Angeles. It preserves the old buildings that give the area its unique character, and for developers like me it is much less expensive to convert offices into lofts than to demolish the building and create something new in its place.

I was the very first person to take advantage of the Adaptive Reuse Ordinance in downtown Los Angeles. Unlike many other buildings that were eligible to be converted, mine was already vacant and I was ready to get moving. All I needed was to hire an architect and come up with a design that I could present to the city, so I immediately found an architect to work with and set to work on those plans. Once I got them approved, I started construction right away.

My original idea for the building was to make it into a hotel, but after talking to hotel chains such as Ramada that had wanted to get into the downtown area and learning that the cost of conversion proved to be too much for them, I gave up on that idea. My next option was to convert the upper floors into lofts and offices and turn the street level into retail businesses.

DREAMS DON'T DIE

From my time growing up in Tel Aviv, I appreciated the combination of residential and business areas. It was the way many streets—in Israel and worldwide—were set up, with shops and restaurants on the street level and apartments above them. Mixed-use buildings give the streets a sense of community rather than the isolated feel of a shopping mall, and this was what I was hoping to see happen in LA's historic downtown.

After the renovations, 639 South Spring Street became Spring Tower Lofts. It's a beautiful building and people love living there. On the street level is LA Cafe, a classy restaurant that uses only fresh and natural ingredients. I wanted the street-level experience to be inviting, and a high-class café is perfect for that location because it caters to everyone and provides a valuable service. It's the restaurant's only location, and people come from all over to eat there. Meanwhile, buildings around my high-rise were also being refurbished, and there was a sense of rebirth and excitement in the old downtown.

The Adaptive Reuse Ordinance is one of the best decisions the city of Los Angeles ever made. Since it was enacted in 1999, it has allowed tens of thousands of lofts, condos, and apartments to be built in the historic downtown and has led to the explosive growth of the area. Once people started moving back, the whole of downtown benefited. Storefronts, cafés, restaurants, and all sorts of other businesses popped up. The area is thriving again, and I am proud to be a part of the revival.

Inspired by the results of the Adaptive Reuse Ordinance, I realized more than ever how important renovation is to

140

the whole of the historic downtown area. Before I finished converting 639 South Spring Street into lofts and new office and retail space, I started looking around for my next project. As it turned out, I didn't have to look far.

CHAPTER 12

EDUCATION
AND TRADITIONS

I dropped out of high school as a sophomore, which doesn't come as a shock to most people who know me well. It's not that they thought I was stupid or incapable of learning; it was just the opposite—they knew I was curious, a go-getter, and a hyper guy who was eager to start making things happen. I just couldn't see the point in sitting in classrooms all day long to study things that didn't interest me when I could be out there doing something useful and making a name for myself.

Make no mistake, I was a terrible student when I was attending school in Israel. I couldn't sit still in class, and I had a hard time concentrating on what the teacher was trying to make us learn that day. In the 1960s and early 1970s when I was in primary school, students like me were called trouble-makers or difficult, and there were no programs designed to help us. The school principal and the teachers just said we were restless kids, and the only thing they did was punish us.

What I soon discovered was that when I made a little bit of noise in the classroom, the teacher would penalize me and put me in the corner. When I made a little bit more noise in the corner, she escorted me out of the classroom and into the hallway so I wouldn't interfere with the other students. From there, I could hang around in the school or in the schoolyard, but I wasn't supposed to leave because there was a fence around the school and the gate was locked.

I wasn't the only kid who was getting kicked out of the classroom, and I soon discovered a small group of trouble-making friends when I was about ten years old. I quickly realized that the teachers were actually giving us an opportunity by throwing us out of class—we could leave the school by climbing over the fence, and we could go to the beach or the park and have fun while the other kids were stuck in the classroom. Later in the day, we'd head back to school and climb over the fence before school was dismissed. Apparently, none of the teachers missed us or realized we were gone because I don't recall ever getting in trouble for leaving the school grounds.

When people saw a couple of ten-year-old kids walking around town or hanging out at the beach in the middle of the day, they'd sometimes ask us, "Shouldn't you be in school?" or "Where are your parents?" I always came up with an excuse, such as we were on our way back to school, but because we didn't cause any trouble and generally kept to ourselves, people didn't pay much attention to us.

One day when I was in the fifth grade and had been kicked out of class, I was hanging around by myself in the schoolyard when I noticed an old woman on the sidewalk on the other side of the fence. She was struggling with her grocery bags and would shuffle for ten or twenty small steps, then put the bags down and stretch out her sore fingers before picking the bags up again and slowly moving another ten or twenty steps. After the second or third time she did this, I jumped over the fence and carried her bags home for her. She was really grateful, but the only reason I was able to help her was because I had been misbehaving and had been removed from the classroom. Afterward, I jumped back over the fence into the schoolyard, like nothing had happened. Unfortunately, skipping school became a regular thing for me.

Later, when I was at Hollywood High, I was bored in class one day and took the opportunity to walk out of the school. Nobody stopped me or questioned me. I just walked out the front door, but a few minutes later a Los Angeles cop saw me and asked, "Hey, kid, what're you doing walking in the street? Why aren't you in school?" I told him I was walking to school, even though I was walking away from the school. He just shrugged his shoulders and went on his way.

I was a bad student, and I'm not proud of that. But I'm in good company. The world is filled with very successful people who never finished high school and who were unable to function well within the confines of a rigid school environment. Richard Branson dropped out of school at sixteen but founded the

145

Virgin brand, became a billionaire, and was knighted by Queen Elizabeth II. The singer Eminem failed ninth grade three times and dropped out of school at seventeen. Kate Moss left school at fourteen to start a modeling career that made her perhaps the most famous supermodel in history. Actors Cameron Diaz, Whoopi Goldberg, and Tom Cruise are three other successful individuals who never completed their schooling.

Benjamin Franklin left school at age ten to work as a soap- and candlemaker, while tech legends Steve Jobs, Bill Gates, and Mark Zuckerberg finished high school but never made it through college. All that said, I don't recommend that others do what I did. Most people who drop out of high school end up living troubled lives. I was very fortunate to get where I am today without even a high school diploma.

* * *

Don't get the impression that I am against school or education. I think it's one of the foundations of civilization and one of society's greatest equalizers. Without education, we can't have true democracy, because a literate and educated voter makes informed decisions for the good of the whole society.

Unlike most people, my education wasn't in the classroom; it came on the streets and in real life. Ever since I dropped out of high school, I have worked hard to educate myself in other ways to make up for what I lost.

I have always been curious, and I learn things in my own

way. I love history, and I enjoy reading books about the people and events that have shaped our world. Like most households when I was growing up, my family had a set of encyclopedias that we kept in the living room—and with so many kids in the house, the books got plenty of use. I was one of those kids whose nose was always in the encyclopedia, learning the things that most interested me—but not necessarily the things my teachers wanted me to learn about—such as the countries of Africa, the life of grizzly bears, and different cultures around the world. Even today, I can spend hours on the Internet, learning new things and keeping up with what's going on in the news.

Back in the 1960s in Israel, there was almost nothing to do during the daytime so kids had to entertain themselves. For me, that usually meant playing with my cousins or riding my bike to the beach or to the swimming pool during the day. At night, we would often go to the movie theater with friends. In between all that, I was passionate about learning and was happy to pull out an encyclopedia and discover something new whenever I was bored.

I never set out with a goal of learning about the Amazon or the Eiffel Tower or George Washington, but when I opened the encyclopedia and saw a picture that caught my attention, it made me want to find out more and I would drift off into that universe. *Who were these people? Why was that mountain important? And why did people want* this *person to lead them instead of* that *guy?*

That's a lot different from a teacher telling you that you

must learn *this* or read *that* chapter. My education was based around learning whatever interested me.

* * *

If I had to do it over again, I probably would have stayed in high school, but I just couldn't do it back in 1975. When I dropped out of Hollywood High, I promised my parents that I would go back to school later to get the education I was missing. So far, I have not been able to fulfill this promise, but I have been able to get an even better education in other ways.

For a while, when I was in my midtwenties, I sat in on some classes at California State University, Northridge, in the San Fernando Valley. I never officially enrolled in the university, but my younger brother Aetan's girlfriend (who later became his wife) was taking classes there, and I thought it would be a good opportunity to tag along with her and learn some new things. I had other friends there as well, and the professors let me sit with my friends to listen to the lectures. I was thirsty for knowledge, and I thought that maybe I had reached the point in my life when I was ready for school again. In total, I sat in on around a dozen classes, mostly history and the liberal arts.

The problem was that I was always busy with work, and by that time I was also a father. I intended to enroll in college and take courses for credit and eventually get my high school diploma and university degree, but I was so occupied with running my businesses, making plans for the next business, and keeping up with my children that I couldn't find time to also be a student.

I sometimes wonder whether I regret not going back to school and not keeping my promise to my parents, because I know that education is very, very important. But at the end of the day, when you're successful and you can do what you want and go where you want, you drive the nicest cars and live in a great house, you marry the most beautiful girl and raise a wonderful family, you realize that life has played out well even without finishing school. In that respect, how can I regret what I did—because everything turned out even better than I could ever have dreamed of when I was fifteen.

Unlike past generations, including that of my own parents, I was also in a fortunate position because I had a choice to go to school or not—and I still have a choice. In my parents' childhood, and for millions of people just like them, it was virtually impossible to get an education because survival meant getting a job and earning a living. The chance for a proper education was never an option. My brother-in-law is my age, and his parents were Holocaust survivors. They were in a concentration camp when they were young, so they never had the opportunity to go to school. They never had a choice—but after the war, they moved to Israel and managed to get some education. For me, it was very different, because I was able to make the choice.

I am often asked if I would prefer to have university degrees but be less successful. I say no; I prefer my life the way I have made it. I got a head start on life, learning a lot and already having successful businesses by the time my peers graduated from university and started working.

On the other hand, it would give me a lot of satisfaction to know that I had put in the work and graduated from a university. In my business, I often deal with lawyers. They are people I have great respect for, because they spent many years going to university and law school before they passed the bar exam and started practicing law. One of the attorneys I was working with found out that I hadn't even completed my sophomore year in high school, and he told me he was amazed at how much I had accomplished in my life. I told him I would trade some of my success for his law degree, and he said he would take that trade any day of the week. It's all based on perspective, but we have to be happy with where we are and what we have managed to achieve, whether that is with an education or with money.

One problem with not having even a high school diploma is that other young people can look at what I have accomplished and use that as a reason to drop out of school, something that I highly do not recommend. All five of my children graduated from high school, but only one graduated from university. The other four did a minimum of two years of college but did not graduate. I was disappointed because they did not have an excuse. Their lives were stable and they were not denied anything, including the best education available to them, so they had no reason not to finish.

I often disagreed with my children over this. They knew

my opinion that education is important, but some of them told me they just couldn't do it and that they had to be allowed to get on with their own lives. I know this is a conversation that millions of other parents have had with their own children, and most of the time, without an education, things do not work out for the best. Fortunately, in my case, it worked out. Some of my children may not have received the education I hoped they would get, but like me, they learned what was essential and became respectful, honest, and very knowledgeable people. In the end, that's all we can hope for.

* * *

Other than my struggles with school, my early life in Tel Aviv was mostly easy and carefree—but it was not religious. Like most of our neighbors and family, we were considered a traditional secular Jewish family. We were like the average Christian in America, who might go to church at Easter and Christmas and prays to God only when the need arises. In that respect, I don't think we were very different from most people in Israel at that time.

Nonetheless, we were aware of our Jewish heritage and were proud to be part of Israel's growth as the Jewish Promised Land. The history of Israel is inextricably tied to religion, and the stereotype is that Israel is full of Orthodox Jews who wear suits, black hats, beards, and yarmulkes, like you might see in certain parts of New York City. The reality is that you barely see people like that in Israel, and the ones you do see are mostly in Jerusalem.

Israelis are no different from anyone else, running the gamut from fervently religious to nonbelievers and those who reject their heritage. My family was somewhere between the two extremes. Like many men in Israel—probably the vast majority—my father didn't go to the synagogue during the week, but he would go to at least one of the three services every Shabbat, the Jewish holy day of rest at the end of the week. Shabbat starts at sundown on Friday and ends when three stars appear in the sky on Saturday evening.

Even though we weren't religious, my family always observed Shabbat at home, and the meal on Friday was a highlight of my life because it was when all the family would get together. I loved seeing my sisters and brothers and cousins and anyone else who joined us. It was like a family reunion with your favorite relatives every week. We'd often get ten, fifteen, or even twenty people around the Shabbat dinner table and sometimes that many for the Shabbat lunch table on Saturday. It was a beautiful experience. It doesn't matter whether you're religious or not—it's a great tradition that connects the family to past generations in a meaningful way. This is why I have tried to continue it with my own family through the years—not for the religious meaning but for the tradition and keeping family close.

We were certainly not Orthodox. Orthodox Jews don't work and don't drive during Shabbat, but we did all that and we went to the beach and lived normal lives. We had fun. We traveled. My parents were open-minded for the sake of their children, and I think they were adapting to the modern world and encouraging us children to explore our own faith and beliefs.

For example, I never wore a yarmulke, and I almost never went to the synagogue, and neither did any of my brothers when they were younger. The only times I can recall going to the synagogue were for the Jewish high holidays such as Rosh Hashanah and Yom Kippur, and in 1972 for my bar mitzvah, the coming-of-age ceremony that marks the transition from boyhood to adulthood at age thirteen. Like every Jewish boy in Israel, I wanted to get to that transition. I'd seen my older brothers and neighbors and cousins go through it, and I wanted to stop being a kid and start being a man like them. It's a very powerful ceremony to go through, and it gives you a new perspective on life.

The other stereotype of Jews is that everyone eats kosher food. The laws of kosher come from the Torah. They outline the foods that Jews can and cannot eat as well as how the food must be prepared. Most Orthodox Jews keep kosher at home, but only a small percentage of Jews overall do it, and I am among the majority who don't require kosher food.

Kosher means "fit" (that is, fit for consumption), but it also means "clean" or "pure," so in addition to food, the term is often used to describe things that are legitimate or legal—and using that definition, I can say honestly that I am 100 percent kosher. I have never committed a crime, I've never been involved in drugs, and I've never stolen a dime from anyone. Every business deal I made was up-front and legal, and every dollar I made was purely clean and kosher.

There is another Hebrew word that sounds almost the same and that describes me even better: *yosher*, which means straight, upright, and morally correct. It refers to what is right, and if I can live the rest of my days being yosher, I think my family can be proud of me.

CHAPTER 13

MY EVEN
MORE INFAMOUS
COUSINS

The fact that I turned out as a reasonably well-adjusted person and have enjoyed a successful and legitimate career may be a little miraculous, considering some of the people in my background. Quite apart from growing up in an illegal casino in Tel Aviv and having my cousin Levi develop from an Israeli bank robber into a major drug lord in Los Angeles—as well as having my own unwanted dealings with gangsters—there is an even more incredible story about my cousins Esther Alon (better known as Etti Alon)and Ofer Maximov.

While Levi's bank robbery shocked Israel, Etti and Ofer caused the downfall of a major Israeli bank, which led to sweeping banking reforms across Israel. Their story commanded headlines and was made into a gripping true crime television drama series.

155

Not long after my family arrived in Los Angeles in the mid-1970s, my mother's brother, Avigdor Maximov, and his family also moved to Los Angeles. My uncle was younger than my brother Jacob and was only about twelve years older than me, and he had three children, including Etti and Ofer.

In addition to being my uncle, Avigdor was one of the biggest gamblers in Israel. One day you might find him with $1 million in his pocket from playing high-stakes poker or black-jack, and another day you'd find him $1 million in debt. He was constantly on the move. He'd lose one of his houses in a card game, but the next time we'd see him, he would have recovered his losses and bought another house. Some of his gambling was in illegal casinos in Israel, but most of the big-time gambling was done in legal casinos overseas. He was just one of those guys who had bad luck or a bad draw of the cards, followed by good fortune—but once he got started gambling, he didn't know how to stop. Thankfully, by the time he came to Los Angeles, his gambling habit appeared to be under control.

This was the uncle I'd brought with me when I signed the lease for my first burger joint—the uncle who'd just arrived from Israel who didn't speak English and who I pretended would be the restaurant's owner. He had a great poker face—for obvious reasons—and he played the part perfectly. After he helped me open my burger joint, he learned English and started a successful business of his own in Los Angeles. Like the rest of us, he was chasing the American Dream. He was happy and stable and even bought a house, but then he started going to the casinos in Las Vegas, which is only about a four-hour drive from LA.

It wasn't long before Avigdor got caught up in the highs and lows of gambling again, and he soon lost everything. Then he won it back, then he lost it again, and so on. He was back to bust or boom, and he packed up his belongings and his family and returned to Israel around 1979.

When my father died in 2002, we honored his wish to be buried in Jerusalem, and a lot of our family members flew there from Los Angeles for the burial. We joined those who were still in Israel, and we rented a bus to take us to the cemetery. As we were driving along the highway, I noticed a line of brand-new Mercedes following the bus. These were top-of-the-line $200,000 cars, but we couldn't figure out who could be that wealthy in Jerusalem and who might be paying their respects to my father.

When we got to the cemetery, it turned out it was my uncle Avigdor and his children, including Etti and Ofer and their families. We knew that Avigdor used to be a huge gambler, but we didn't know he was back to his old gambling habits. After the funeral, when we were having a huge dinner with all the family and friends, my sister Sephora asked Avigdor's wife, Rachel, "What lottery did you guys win?"

Rachel's reply was chilling. "We didn't win the lottery," she said. "We are all in deep, deep trouble. You'll hear about it soon."

When Sephora told me this, I was really curious about what was going on, so I asked my uncle about it. He gave me the same answer: "We can't talk about it. You will hear about it before too long."

* * *

Less than a month later when we were back in Los Angeles, we found out on the news that Etti and Ofer, along with my uncle Avigdor, had been arrested in Israel for embezzling 250 million shekels—or about $60 million—from the bank where Etti worked. The news reported that Etti had stolen the money to finance her brother's gambling habits.

It turned out that Ofer was an even bigger gambler than his father, Avigdor. Ofer was traveling all over the world to gamble and was well known in the biggest casinos in Macau, Las Vegas, and Monte Carlo. He was a "high roller" who gambled with millions of dollars, and what he was doing was ten times bigger than anything his father ever did. His nickname was the "King of the Casinos."

Ofer's sister Etti was the deputy head of investments at Trade Bank in Tel Aviv, and we learned that she had been stealing money from customers' accounts and giving the money to her brother. Trade Bank was established in the mid-1930s and was one of Israel's oldest and most trusted banks, so the news was shocking and took everyone completely by surprise.

The way Etti had accomplished this was astonishingly simple. She was essentially running a variation on a Ponzi scheme. She would take money from one customer's account, but when the customer asked for their balance, she would take money from another account to make it seem like everything was OK. Nobody was any the wiser. The customers' balances appeared to be correct, and she was so thorough and so careful that the bank did not have a clue that she was siphoning off literally millions of dollars every year over a five-year period from 1997 to 2002. She gave this money to Ofer so that he could pay off his debts and continue to gamble with the biggest players in Monte Carlo and Las Vegas.

Of course, Etti knew that what she was doing was stealing and that it was illegal, and one day the weight of the guilt became too much for her to bear. She went to one of the most well-known attorneys in Israel and confessed to him what she had done. She told him the whole story, from beginning to end, including the fact that she was giving the money to her brother to feed his gambling addiction. It was an incredible story—and it was so unbelievable that the attorney started laughing.

"Are you telling me about a movie you watched," he asked her, "or is this for real?"

"It's 100 percent for real," she told him.

"If it's for real, and if you stole as much money as I think you're talking about, how come the bank hasn't noticed?"

She had no answer, except that she had done a great job covering her tracks. Slowly, the attorney started to think she may be telling the truth, and he told her they had to go to the police.

Together, Etti and the attorney went to the police fraud

squad headquarters in Tel Aviv, where she repeated her story. Like the attorney, the police started laughing. They didn't believe it was possible to steal millions of dollars from a bank without anyone noticing, but Etti insisted it was true. Finally, one of the police officers told her, "Look, I'm going to call the bank manager and see what he says."

Just like everyone else, the bank manager refused to believe it when he was told what my cousin claimed. "She's dreaming," he said. "I would know if she had stolen even one shekel, and I can tell you that the bank would have shut down long ago if a quarter of a billion shekels were missing."

Less than twenty-four hours later, the bank realized that Etti was telling the truth, and it shut its doors. Etti and my uncle Avigdor were arrested. Ofer was gambling at a casino in Romania at the time, but there was an international warrant out for his arrest and eventually he was arrested and extradited to Israel.

* * *

According to news reports, Ofer had run up huge gambling debts with organized crime figures, and the money that Etti had stolen from Trade Bank was meant to repay some of these debts. It was also reported that Ofer still owed the underworld figures as much as 100 million shekels at the time of his arrest and that he was being extorted and threatened unless he paid back the loans, plus considerable interest. The amount was so enormous that, according to Israeli police sources, it redrew the map of organized crime in Israel and transformed some small-time thugs into crime kingpins.

Etti went on trial in 2002 and was found guilty. She was sentenced to seventeen years in prison and a five-million-shekel fine. The judge recognized that Etti was a victim who had been trapped emotionally because of her devotion to her brother. During her trial, she told the court that she had stolen the money to save her brother's life, claiming that unless he paid back his loans, the criminal gangs would kill him. "Every day he came to me with a new story," she said—but she could not go to the police, because the gangs would kill his whole family, including her. The whole operation was so secretive that even Etti's husband knew nothing about it and suspected nothing. Etti herself didn't keep any of the money, so there were no tell-tale signs such as expensive clothes or jewelry.

"One day, Ofer came to me with his shirt ripped and shoes with no laces," she stated. "He said his threateners had tied the laces around his neck and showed him a revolver. They threatened him that the next time he did not pay back his debts, they would hang him. Ofer came to me to ask for money and said he had nowhere else to go."

Even so, Ofer never stopped gambling and never stopped taking out riskier and riskier loans, and eventually Etti had no choice but to put an end to it. "I could have fled the country with my children and taken another two or three million shekels overseas," she testified. "I didn't do so, because I wanted to be caught."

Shortly after her conviction, Etti asked the bank to release her pension, which had built up to 67,000 shekels, to support her children. The bank refused, claiming the money should be used to make restitution for the 250 million shekels she had stolen from the bank's customers.

Ofer went on trial separately and was also found guilty. He was sentenced to fifteen years in prison, which was extended to eighteen years when the prosecution appealed to Israel's Supreme Court for a harsher sentence. While he admitted in court that he was addicted to gambling, his defense was that he claimed he never knew the money Etti gave him was stolen. Instead, he said he believed it was a legitimate loan, and that he'd paid back every penny he'd "borrowed" from her.

Ofer said in court that he lost up to 100,000 shekels (about $25,000) every day because of his gambling. He traveled to London, Monte Carlo, and other places around the world, going from casino to casino in an effort to find credit and to change his luck. Often he gambled only for a few hours before flying home. As his losses mounted and the pressure to repay the loans increased, he allegedly even thought of committing suicide.

The judge, Shlomo "Shelly" Timan, said that he did not believe a word that came out of Ofer's mouth. He called him a "liar unable to utter a word of truth" and added that it was "hard to believe that Ofer Maximov and Etti Alon are both children of the same parents."

The police and banking authorities believed Etti and Ofer's

father, my uncle Avigdor, was responsible for helping them launder the money and move it between accounts, and he was also found guilty in a separate trial. Avigdor was sentenced to six years in prison and a one-million-shekel fine, and he suffered a stroke from all the stress while serving his sentence.

The embezzlement had far-reaching effects beyond just my cousins and my uncle. First, the whole affair destroyed public trust in banks in Israel. People were furious that the entire banking system had allowed such obvious and egregious fraud to take place. Fortunately for Trade Bank's customers, the money was insured by the Israeli government, which reimbursed almost all of the 250 million shekels that had been stolen.

Meanwhile, the bank collapsed and went out of business, but the bank's officials and board members did not get off lightly. They were fined eighteen million shekels for their carelessness in allowing this to happen under their control. The bank's auditors, Kesselman & Kesselman accounting firm, found itself in trouble as well. The firm was found guilty of negligence and ordered to pay a twenty-million-shekel fine.

The case also exposed illegal gambling in Israel. Ofer had run up gambling debts with several large illegal casinos that were run by organized crime, and the crime bosses were indicted, which had the effect of shutting down their businesses and temporarily bringing the illegal gambling business in Israel to a halt. These casinos were big-time, not like the small eight-table casino that my brother used to run in the back of my mother's restaurant in Tel Aviv.

More widespread, the crime families that Ofer was involved with used the millions of dollars in profits they had gained from Ofer to expand their money-laundering and drug empires around the world. They diverted this so-called gray money into operations in Tel Aviv and Los Angeles and many places in between. One of the "gray market" dealers, Benny Revizada, used the money he got from Ofer to buy apartments and strengthen his ownership stake in the Maccabi Jaffa soccer club in Israel.

Once it left Ofer's hands, most of the ill-gotten money passed through several secret accounts before it reached its final destination, so it proved almost impossible for the police to trace it. Getting it back was even harder, but the authorities nonetheless managed to recover about forty million shekels.

A direct result of the crimes committed by my cousins Etti and Ofer was that international crime bosses were exposed. Disputes over the millions of shekels spawned a series of gang wars between rival crime bosses that lasted for years. Members of the Abergil and Abutbul families in Israel were arrested, along with many others who were connected to the case.

Another outcome was a complete overhaul of the Israeli banking system. Etti's crime spree revealed one of the weaknesses in the system: she was responsible for approving both credits and deposits, so new regulations were put in place that prohibited one employee from overseeing all aspects of an account. The more eyes on an account, the less chance there would be for fraud.

New regulations also forced all bank employees to take vacations. One of the ways Etti managed to keep her thefts secret was that she never took a vacation, thereby preventing a temporary replacement from seeing the illegal transactions. What's more, Etti was able to keep stealing money for five years because she held the same position at the bank all that time and nobody else had access to her accounts. Banks put a policy in place to start rotating employees in key positions to prevent just one person from accessing an account.

* * *

In August 2016, Etti was released from the Neve Tirtza women's prison after serving a little more than fourteen years of her seventeen-year sentence. She was no longer considered a danger to the public. Ofer was released from prison one year early in November 2019.

The release of my cousins should have been the end of the story, but it turned out to be a new beginning. Their story was so compelling in Israel and both Etti and Ofer were so infamous that enterprising television producers realized there was potential in turning their story into a television series.

Based on the story of my cousins and uncle, yes Studios, one of the major production companies in Israel, developed *Me'ila* (which means "betrayal" in Hebrew) as a seven-part weekly series of forty-five-minute episodes. The show began airing on July 29, 2021, and it captivated Israel. It is a more or less faithful retelling of the facts, with some fictional elements thrown in for dramatic effect. The final episode, which first aired on September 9, 2021, ended with the trials of Etti and Ofer.

Actress Dana Ivgy played my cousin Etti and won the Best Actress in a Drama Series award from the Israeli Television Academy, while Yehuda Levi—one of Israel's most famous actors—played my cousin Ofer.

Me'ila was hugely successful in Israel, and it was also released as a streaming series in the United States under the title *Embezzlement*. The name reminds me that I have been surrounded by a bunch of criminals throughout my life—but also that my story is totally different from others in my family, and that I got where I am today without stealing from anyone and without sending anyone to prison.

CHAPTER 14

THE SCRIPT

I have always loved movies. Even though there were periods in my life when I didn't have time to go to the movie theater or follow the new releases, I always eventually caught up on them. It was harder to do this before the Internet, of course, because you had to keep track of the TV listings and hope something you'd been wanting to see would come on, or search through the stacks at a video store like Blockbuster, but I was determined to see all of the best films.

My favorite movie of all time is *Goodfellas,* the 1990 film directed by Martin Scorsese. The movie was based on the true story of a New York Mafia family as told by writer Nicholas Pileggi in his bestselling book *Wiseguy,* and it brought together some of the greatest actors of all time—Robert De Niro, Ray Liotta, Paul Sorvino, Joe Pesci, and Lorraine Bracco. I must have seen *Goodfellas* a dozen times or more.

One day I started to realize that my own life had quite a few dramatic moments and movie-worthy scenes. It was nothing like the drama, deception, and betrayal of *Goodfellas*, but the more I thought about it, the more it seemed like my early life had played out as if it were a movie. People had been telling me this for years, but it wasn't until I was old enough to look back on my life and to assess the path I had taken that I realized they were right. I thought I had a good story to tell, not just about myself but also about my family.

I also had begun to realize that so much of my life was about right and wrong—and about the decisions that had put me on the right track. There were so many times I could have followed my cousin Levi or my cousin Ofer into a life of crime, but that's not the way things played out.

I was fortunate to live in Los Angeles, a city that was built around the film and television industry, and to be in a business where I occasionally ran into high-powered movie people, from directors and producers to actors and scriptwriters and everyone in between. I also had some contacts in the movie business from renting my buildings to production companies, and I became intrigued with the idea of turning my story into a movie.

One day I ran into screenwriter Michael Micco and mentioned my idea to him. He loved it, and we met numerous times to talk about my story. Several months later, we had written a movie script that followed my journey from the illegal casino in Tel Aviv, to Levi's bank robbery, to my family coming to Los Angeles, to my burger joints and auto shops, and ending with Levi falling into the drug trade, his death, and Jacob and me recovering the money that he'd hidden in New York so we could get Yoni released.

At that point a second writer, Jenna Mattison, became involved. She honed the script and got it ready to show to producers—and she loved it so much that she became a producer herself.

It was at about this point that we settled on the title *For the Love of Money*. This comes from 1 Timothy 6:10 in the Bible: "For the love of money is the root of all evil"—which is also the first line of dialogue in the movie. This is an appropriate title, because money by itself is a necessity and can be used for the benefit of humankind, but when it is coveted and misused, it always leads to trouble. Many of the bad things I have seen in my life have been the result—either direct or indirect—of people making bad choices about money.

It was important to me that the movie showed not only how I navigated my way through life and found success but how essential it is for all of us to pick the correct path and opt for the right way to succeed.

After about a year, we had the script ready, and the story of my life was on its way to becoming a movie!

* * *

It was exciting to put my life story down on paper and to think that it could really come to life on the big screen. I was proud of the direction my life had taken, and it gave me a good feeling that the message I wanted to get out there was also the recipe for my success.

In the movie, the person who chose the right way in life established legitimate and profitable businesses, got married to a beautiful girl, had a family, and succeeded in life. The one who chose the wrong way went to prison, was never fully happy, and ended up being filled with bullet holes. The message of the movie was that going the legitimate and honest way is the correct way.

I wanted to get that message across not through moralizing or telling people to follow one religion or another, but through action. Most people are visual learners, and showing them causes and effects in a series of dramatic scenes can have much more impact than a dry and meaningless lecture. That's the beauty of movies—they're not just for entertainment; they can help make the world a better place if the message is communicated in the right way.

I had been telling my friends and family for years about my decisions to follow the right path at every stage of my life, and they're the ones who encouraged me to get that message out to a wider audience. I'm not sure they ever thought my story would be made into a movie, but without their support it probably never would have happened.

As I was developing the idea for the movie, I met a number of movie producers in Los Angeles, and they liked the story I was trying to tell. They introduced me to other moviemakers who they thought might be interested, but the first thing these other producers wanted to do was to alter the story. They told me that if they were going to be involved with the movie, they would do it their way, which meant coming up with a new script and changing the storylines. It would be based on my life, but it wouldn't necessarily reflect my life.

They thought it would make a better story if my wife cheated on me with Levi. They said it would create a great conflict point in the story if Aline fell for the criminal instead of the one who took the right path. It would be more "market-able" that way because, they claimed, people wanted to see a woman cheating on her honorable husband by going off with the bad boy. I told them, "Hell no, I don't want that. I will never allow this to be in my script. That's not my story. It may work for someone else, but it doesn't work for me." They wanted the story to be more like *Goodfellas* or a gangster movie.

I know most movies are an illusion. Even when the story is 100 percent based on the truth, there will still be an element of fiction to it. Actors are playing roles, and the words are made up to tell the story in the best way possible, but I saw no reason to invent new stories or introduce new conflicts when the true story was good enough to stand on its own. What the producers were asking for was that I create a fiction about my own life for the sake of selling a movie, but I wasn't about to do that.

I lived close to Hollywood and have always been a huge movie fan, but it still surprised me that a good story isn't always what the directors and producers think is enough to sell a movie. There are a lot of ingredients that make a movie more sellable, but there was no way I was going to change my story to the extent that it was no longer recognizable.

The first line that comes on the screen at the start of the movie is, "Based on a true story." Unless it's a documentary, no movie can be an absolutely true story—but I was trying to tell the right story in the right way, not to create a different illusion. I also wanted to make a movie that I could enjoy with my family and friends.

Instead of letting a bunch of strangers have control of my story, I ended up being the major producer and spending almost $5 million of my own money to make the movie. While that sounds like a huge sum of money, in Hollywood $5 million is not considered a big-budget movie.

I was extremely fortunate to be able to walk away from negotiations with the producers, make a good movie, and finance it my way with my money. The average person who has an extraordinary story to tell is unlikely to have my resources and will be at the mercy of the people who want to change the story to sell more tickets and more downloads. Thankfully, that wasn't the case with my movie.

* * *

Once the prospect of making my movie began to take shape, I started looking for and interviewing the right people to put in charge, starting with a director. Through various connections, I became acquainted with Ellie Kanner, an up-and-coming director who had expressed interest in directing my movie. She was married to David Zuckerman, the writer and television producer who was well known for his work on TV shows such as *The Fresh Prince of Bel-Air, King of the Hill, American Dad!,* and *Family Guy.*

Ellie had a long history in television and movies, most notably as an award-winning casting director for shows such as *The Drew Carey Show, Sabrina the Teenage Witch, Sex and the City,* and *Friends.* She directed her first films, *Rachel's Room* with Maggie Grace and *Italian Ties* with Scott Baio, in 2001, and her most recent work before I hired her were some television shows and the movie *Wake* with Bijou Phillips.

In retrospect, I probably should have designated more money in the budget for a bigger-name director. A certain percentage of the movie audience goes to a movie based on the director, so names such as Martin Scorsese or Steven Spielberg or Quentin Tarantino pretty much guarantee a wide release and greater publicity. If Scorsese or Tarantino had directed my movie, it would have generated $100 million in sales. I should have known this because of my real estate background. When you build a new structure and use a famous architect, that architect's name alone adds value to the building in the same way that a director's name adds value to a movie.

Kanner was not in the top tier of well-known directors—but in reality, people such as Scorsese, Spielberg, and Tarantino are very selective about the movies they make, and they charge top dollar. The vast majority of Hollywood movies were made by "unknown" directors and ones who were building experience, and I chose not to spend millions for a big-time director because I wanted to stick to my budget.

The actors in a movie are usually an even greater draw than the director, and I was fortunate to get some of my heroes to be in my movie. The biggest name was James Caan, who played the character of the gangster Micky. Caan made his name in television in the early 1960s before going into movies, and he really exploded onto the scene in 1972 as Sonny Corleone in *The Godfather*, a role that earned him Academy Award and Golden Globe nominations.

I am often asked how I managed to get a major star like Caan in my movie. He was free to pick and choose what he wanted to do, and every filmmaker and producer would have loved to get him. I'd never met him before the movie started shooting, so it's not like he owed me a favor or anything like that. He told me the reason he decided to do my movie was that he loved the script and wanted to be part of it. It was as simple as that, and I was flattered that he saw the potential.

Other A-list actors in the film were Jeffrey Tambor, who at the time was playing George Bluth Sr. and Oscar Bluth in *Arrested Development*, as the real estate broker Mr. Solomon; Edward Furlong, who played the hoodlum Tommy; Steven Bauer, who took the role of the Colombian drug lord; and Paul Sorvino, another of my favorite actors who played Paul Cicero in *Goodfellas* and who had a small scene in my movie as a corrupt priest. It was also very important to get the right actress to play Aline, my wife. That person proved to be French actress Delphine Chanéac, who perfectly captured Aline's beauty and character.

Two of the big-name actors, Edward Furlong and Steven Bauer, were going through problems with drugs, and it was rumored that they were not reliable. Furlong was known for playing John Connor, the child in *Terminator 2: Judgment Day*, while Bauer's most famous role was as Manny Ray, Al Pacino's right-hand man in *Scarface*. Most producers and directors weren't willing to take a chance on them, which meant that they were not expensive to hire. I rolled the dice, and I had no problems. They were great to work with and were just right for my movie.

Probably the biggest challenge was finding the right actors to play me. It is, to say the least, a strange experience to look at lists of actors and go through auditions with them to find the ones you think are most like you and can tell your story the best. It's not necessarily about how they look but more about their demeanor and the image they project. I didn't want someone who was perceived as aggressive or angry, but someone I could identify with.

For the young Izek in the early scenes in Tel Aviv, we hired the incredibly talented Cody Anthony, known then as Cody Longo. He was very comfortable in the role, and he had a lot of confidence.

The older version of me was played by the Israeli actor Yehuda Levi—or Yuda Levi, as he went by in the movie credits— who was well known in Israel for his television work and was an award-winner for playing the role of Jagger in the movie *Yossi & Jagger*. In fact, he was one of the most famous actors in Israel, and people called him the "Tom Cruise of Israel."

In order for Yehuda to get to know me better, he actually moved into my house before the movie was shot. He lived with us for several weeks so he could see how I behaved and how I walked and talked. He ate breakfast with me and came to my office to observe me at work, and in the evenings he had supper with me, so he was with me all day and got to know me very well. Consequently, he was able to mimic me almost exactly.

There were exceptions, though. One day while he was following me around, he started walking in a funny way. I was taken aback, so I asked him, "Is that how I walk? Are you imitating me?"

He started laughing and told me, "No, I'm exaggerating a bit. I was trying to walk like a gangster."

"Wait a minute," I told him. "I'm not the gangster. I'm the good guy in this movie!"

Through a strange twist of fate, Yehuda Levi also had a small role in the 2005 movie *Munich*, which was directed by Steven Spielberg and followed the events of the massacre of Israeli athletes and officials at the 1972 Olympic Games in Munich. If not for dumb luck or stupidity, my brother Abe would have been one of the Israeli athletes whose story was told in the movie. Even more incredibly, Yehuda also ended up playing my cousin Ofer Maximov in the Israeli television series *Me'ila* in 2021. The crazy thing was, he had no idea when he was cast that Ofer was my cousin.

Another key person I hired was cinematographer Andrzej

Sekula, who had shot *Pulp Fiction* and *Reservoir Dogs*. The cinematographer, also known as the director of photography, is responsible for setting up the shots and deciding on the most appropriate lighting and sound for each scene. After the director, the cinematographer is probably the most important crew member. Sekula is an incredible talent, and his gritty style helped give my movie the look and feel of classic gangster movies like *Goodfellas* and *The Godfather*.

Altogether, the actors—known as "talent" in the industry—cost me about $700,000, a significant portion of the budget for the movie. But without the actors, there would be no movie. My original budget for Caan was $150,000 for two days of work, but he was a bit more expensive than I originally anticipated, so I ended up paying him $250,000.

Once everything was set—the script was written, the director was in place, and the actors were ready—we could finally start on the production. My movie was actually being made!

CHAPTER 15

FOR THE LOVE OF MONEY

I have always taken pride in being able to find the right people to make my visions a reality, but I have also been very much involved in every step of the process. I hire the best architects and the best designers, but I make my own changes to the designs and I tell them the way I want things done. It's always a collaborative effort, but it has my fingerprints all over it.

It was the same with my movie, *For the Love of Money*. When I first started the project, I did not realize what an important role the director had. As a movie fan, I intuitively knew a lot of what the director's job was and I could tell one director's work from another's, but it was not until I was on the movie set and watching what happens on a day-to-day basis that I understood just how vital a director is to literally every part of the film.

Production on *For the Love of Money* started in October

2010, and unfortunately, I immediately started seeing things that should have been done differently or that didn't live up to my vision. Just as with any of my businesses, that's where I stepped in—this time as the movie's producer.

On several occasions, I moved the director aside because what I was witnessing on the set was not what I had in mind for how the scene should be shot. I told the director I was going to do it my own way, and I basically directed some of the scenes. I'd spent good money to get great actors like James Caan and Paul Sorvino, so I wanted to make sure the story was told in the right way.

At the very beginning of the production, I was concerned that the actor playing the adult version of me, Yehuda Levi, was overacting. He had spent several weeks living in my house and following me around, and he got most of my mannerisms right, but he didn't see that I was always calm and in control. I told him to relax, because I didn't feel comfortable with him acting so high-strung, and I didn't feel like it was an accurate portrayal of me. Once he relaxed, it was just right.

Working on the film was an eye-opening experience because the same lines can come across so differently depending on how the actors and director approach the scene. I know that if I had given control only to the director and not been on the set myself, I never would have been able to correct these scenes and people would have walked away with the wrong impression of me.

* * *

The first scene in *For the Love of Money* shows a younger version of me and a younger version of Yoni racing a pair of red Ferraris along Mulholland Drive, one of the most scenic and iconic roads in Los Angeles. Yoni and I often dreamed about doing something like this, and it is the one part of the movie that drifts into fantasy rather than reality. The very last scene in the movie continues the race, so it more or less brings the story full circle and into the present.

The way that car racing scene was shot was cool. To get the right feel of speed and danger, Mulholland Drive was shut down to traffic and we had the cameraman ride in the sidecar of a motorcycle that raced along with the cars. There were two professional stunt drivers, but I didn't like the way one of them was driving, so I ended up driving one of the cars myself for some of the shots. Except for the close-ups of the actors playing Yoni and me, you can't tell who's driving, but I know it was me driving one of those cars. It was important to me to get the racing scenes right, and being able to drive fast in Los Angeles—and in a Ferrari, no less!—and have the freedom of the road was a thrill that will stay with me forever.

There were several other parts of the movie that I also took control of. One was the first major scene in the movie, in which my cousin Levi robs the bank in Israel. Another was the scene where Paul Sorvino, the drug-dealing priest, is shot

181

in his church. The director originally filmed the scene to show Sorvino getting shot and falling down, then it moved on to the next scene.

To me, that was not satisfactory and a little boring. I wanted it to be a bit more dramatic, so I directed the scene that was shown in the movie. In the scene, Sorvino falls on his back and looks up at the beautiful dome in the church. I thought there was a production value in the dome, so I wanted the viewer to see what Sorvino saw as he was lying on the ground and getting dizzier.

Another scene I ended up directing was when my cousin Levi got killed. Nobody witnessed the killing, but I wanted to get the action as close as possible to what I had understood it to be.

Although nobody knows for sure, in my opinion there were probably four shooters. Everything happened so quickly, including the getaway, and Levi had at least a hundred bullets in his body, so the shooting must have been done by more than one or two people with assault rifles or machine guns. It happened on the street outside Yoni's home. Levi had just made a quick visit to Yoni's house, and Yoni was sitting in his house when he heard the gunshots. When he ran outside, all he saw was the car with Levi's bullet-riddled body in it. In just a matter of seconds, the assassins had disappeared.

I wanted that scene to suggest the speed and brutality of the killing, so I directed the van to pull up as soon as the shooting stopped so it could whisk the assassins away before anyone could tell what had happened.

Perhaps because it was all so new to me, I loved being on the set and watching the process of a movie being made. For someone who'd lived vicariously through the movies for so long, it was fascinating to realize that a ninety-minute show is the end result of a process that takes years to complete. Every step along the way was fun and exciting, from writing the first words of the script to getting the film editor's last approval.

It was also novel for me to see how actors work on a set. James Caan and Paul Sorvino were so experienced that everything was second nature to them. They immediately understood the characters they were playing and the way I wanted them to be shown. Once they were in character, they didn't need instruction. The director tried to tell them what to do and where to stand and how to say the lines, but really what she needed to do was just move to the side and let them take over. They added their own ideas and ended up doing things their own way, but that only made the movie better. That's the power of great acting, and I was fortunate to get two of the best actors in the business to work on my movie.

* * *

From writing the script to finishing the editing, the whole process took a couple of years to complete, but shooting the movie wrapped in twenty-eight days. For a film like this with so many scenes and so many locations, it seems like a miracle that everything was done within that twenty-eight-day period. This came down to good management and hiring the right people who scheduled everything in the right order and had everything in place and ready to go on day one. By the time the actors arrived on the set and the cameras started rolling, nothing was left to chance. There would be no surprises.

The main shock to me was that it was so expensive to make a movie, even a so-called low-budget one. I spent almost $3 million just on that twenty-eight-day period—and I was warned that going beyond twenty-eight days would be exponentially more expensive, maybe half a million dollars a day more expensive. One reason was that many of the actors and crew members were already booked for other jobs after this one, and if my movie went beyond schedule, I would either have to pay huge penalties to get the people I wanted or find last-minute replacements at a higher cost. Fortunately, that didn't happen, but we used every minute of those twenty-eight days we had available.

If you look at the credits at the end of *For the Love of Money*—or any Hollywood movie—you'll see there are hundreds of people and companies involved in the production. We think of a movie being about the actors, directors, and camerapeople, but there are so many other essential departments, such as lighting and sound, stunts, set design, and costume and makeup, as well as things such as transportation and trailers for the actors and catering three meals a day on the set for all those people.

It all added up quickly, and everyone had to be paid in accordance with union rules. No significant movie—even one on a budget like we had—could be made in Los Angeles unless it was done with union workers.

One expense we did not have to worry about was paying for locations to shoot the various scenes. I saved money on that because we made good use of my own property in Los Angeles, where most of the movie was set. Many of the scenes were shot on locations that I owned, and even the farmers market outside the bank that Levi robbed was an alley in downtown Los Angeles that I controlled because I owned the buildings surrounding it.

I had a budget, so I knew pretty much what the movie was going to cost before we even set foot on the set. Even so, there were some shocks. Early in the process, the director and one of the other producers came to me and told me they needed another five trailers for makeup and other things. Each trailer can cost thousands of dollars to rent, even for a short time, but not having the trailers could potentially have caused more problems than we expected and could have even delayed the movie and pushed it into twenty-nine or thirty days of production. I wasn't happy about shelling out an extra $40,000 for more trailers, but in the end, it was the right thing to do because it kept us on track.

Even though we shot the movie entirely in Los Angeles, where movies are made all the time and you would think people would take it in stride, there were always a few people who wanted to interfere and who bugged the actors and the crew. We dealt with these things very diplomatically. This was a period movie that took place in the 1970s and 1980s, so all the cars had to be from the right era. A few days before we shot certain scenes, we put up notices saying that parking was not allowed on certain days. Some people left their cars on the street anyway, so we had to tow a few away. There were also one or two people who must have been through this before, because they wanted to be paid to move their cars—and they got $100 just to drive their cars to the next street.

Despite our best efforts, there were inevitably some cars and other landmarks that were not correct, so these had to be fixed in postproduction. There are people who can make a new car look vintage and can change a twenty-first-century background to make it look like the 1970s. It's quite amazing, but it comes at a cost.

Once the movie was shot and the production team left, the movie went into postproduction. This process included editing, and it cost another couple million dollars. Just like the other parts of moviemaking, I was intrigued with what took place over the course of another several months before we had what we considered to be the finished movie.

I spent quite a bit of time in the studio with the film's editor, Eric Strand, who polished the movie and cut it to ninety-three minutes. There were so many decisions that had to be made in the editing room. The movie that we shot was way too long and had too many scenes, so we had to decide what scenes could be cut—and even what lines within scenes could be cut—without affecting the story or creating holes in the narrative.

Even so, there were scenes in the script that never even got shot, like the time Yoni and I took the pigeons from my grandfather's neighbor's house. In that case, we already knew the movie would be too long without that scene and it would probably get cut later anyway, so we made the decision that it wasn't essential to the story and chose not to spend valuable time filming it.

* * *

One of the most important parts of *For the Love of Money* is the music, which was added in the editing process. For me, the music had to evoke the era of my youth, and it had to be authentic. It was the soundtrack of my life and of my generation.

As the producer, I insisted on using only the genuine music, which was an extra expense but one that I thought was necessary. Using the original artists' music was costly, and I spent about $300,000 to purchase the rights to use the songs.

The movie starts with "Ramble Tamble," a 1970 song written by John Fogerty and performed by Creedence Clearwater Revival. The song plays over the opening credits and into the scene of my cousin Yoni and me racing Ferraris down Mulholland Drive.

There are two dozen songs in the movie, some of which are just short snippets of the songs. Every song was selected because it complemented what was going on in the movie at that time—and it was a song that might have been playing when the action was taking place in real life. After "Ramble Tamble" comes "Joy to the World" by Three Dog Night, "Spirit in the Sky" by Norman Greenbaum, and "20th Century Boy" by T. Rex.

Other songs included "Magic Carpet Ride" by Steppenwolf, "Call Me" by Blondie, and "In the Air Tonight" by Phil Collins. The movie ends, appropriately, with "For the Love of Money," the classic 1973 O'Jays hit as performed by The Hit Co. while the closing credits roll. Not only does the song match the movie's title, but it's a fabulous piece of music that hit the radio at about the time I arrived in Los Angeles.

* * *

It probably goes without saying that I was a nervous wreck in the days before *For the Love of Money* made its theatrical debut. It opened in Los Angeles and New York on Friday, June 8, 2012, but it became real when I looked in the *New York Times* in May 2012 and saw the June movie release schedule:

FOR THE LOVE OF MONEY 20 years in the life of an Israeli immigrant (Yuda Levi) whose pursuit of the American dream includes involvement with a gangster (James Caan) and a Colombian drug lord (Steven Bauer).

That may not have been how I would have summarized the movie, but there it was in black and white: a listing in the *New York Times*. People were being asked to pay good money for the chance to get an insight into my own life. On the same day, there were several other movies released to the theaters, including *Madagascar 3, Safety Not Guaranteed,* and Ridley Scott's *Prometheus. Men in Black 3* and *Snow White and the Huntsman* had been out for a while and were still playing to full houses.

The day before the movie opened, *The Hollywood Reporter*—a magazine devoted to the Hollywood film industry—ran a review of *For the Love of Money* by Frank Scheck. It was mostly positive, especially pointing out James Caan and the "delicious supporting cast." The review also noted that the "gritty cinematography," "fluid editing," and "vintage '70s pop hits on the soundtrack" gave it an impressive look and sound. In other words, it was exactly what I was hoping for. Most people, including the reviewer, were surprised at the quality of the cinematography and the lineup of A-list actors that I'd managed to secure for a movie on a limited budget.

The premiere of *For the Love of Money* in Los Angeles was quite an affair, and it was a thrill for everyone in my family, along with my friends, to be part of a red-carpet event and to see the finished movie. We had about eight hundred people at the premiere, including all the stars from the movie. It was huge!

When I saw the finished movie for the first time in the theater, I enjoyed it immensely because I knew I was watching a true story; even better, I was surrounded by my family and friends. By the time the credits started to roll at the end of the movie, I was a happy guy. I was satisfied that I had managed to tell my story and to get my message across. The only thing I questioned was whether it could have been a little better and a little more exciting if I had spent the extra money on a director with more experience.

A lot of my friends and business associates saw the movie, and many of them had no idea beforehand that my life was so complex and intriguing. I think they saw me in a different way—hopefully in a better way—after the movie. My family members who were portrayed in the story loved it as well, although by that time Levi's widow and three daughters had moved back to Israel and I hadn't kept in contact with them.

On the day the movie opened, the *New York Times* ran a review of the film—but it wasn't quite as flattering. The main problem that reviewer Neil Genzlinger had was not with the story or the actors but instead with the premise—a good guy winning instead of falling into the trap of criminal behavior. He'd rather watch a movie "centered on the guys committing the crimes."

I guess this reviewer wanted to see the good guy's wife have an affair with one of the bad boys and to see me become a criminal—exactly what the potential producers at the start of the process had wanted, instead of an authentic story of how choosing the right path can lead to success. In my opinion, this reviewer missed the point of the movie.

Also on June 8, the *Los Angeles Times* ran a review by Gary Goldstein that called attention to the movie's "quick pacing, technical proficiency and an enjoyable use of popular period tunes." I was glad to see that the music met with approval once again.

The official poster for *For the Love of Money* showed the three biggest stars at the top—James Caan, Paul Sorvino, and Edward Furlong (looking menacing and holding a gun)—with the Los Angeles skyline in the background. The bottom half showed the bank heist scene with guns blazing. The movie's title in the middle included the tagline, "Based on a true story."

I can see why the distributors chose those images for the poster, and in a way, I suppose Hollywood won the battle I'd been fighting against. I'd fought to tell my story and to make it as truthful as possible, and that was, in fact, the movie that was made. The poster, however, was selling the three stars and giving the impression that it was a film about crime. By the time the poster was designed, my role was pretty much over and the movie was in the hands of the distributors, who thought they knew what people wanted to see and tailored the poster accordingly. A second poster was also made, but that one focused even more on the bank robbery and featured Levi in his mask during the holdup.

To illustrate another disconnect between the movie and the marketing, the IMDb page for the movie includes this summary: "One man leaves his old gangster lifestyle for a fresh start. As his past creeps up, he'll have to protect his family, even if it means going back to his old ways." IMDb is the go-to resource for everything about movies, but I don't know where this description came from—because it is not what the movie is about! I never had a "gangster lifestyle," so I couldn't make a decision about going back to those "old ways." The summary

191

seems to be mixing my character and Levi's into one person. Maybe that's how movies are sold, but anyone who watches the movie will never come away with that conclusion.

On June 28, about three weeks after it opened in the United States, *For the Love of Money* had another red-carpet premiere in Israel, where it opened with the Hebrew title *Be'shem ha'kesef.* The movie was very successful in Israel and ran in the theaters there for a long time. The DVD was first released in the US in September, and in early 2013 the DVD was made available in Europe, where it was called *The Money*. In Japan, it was called *Gang in LA*—making the focus on criminals even greater. The Japanese DVD cover highlighted Edward Furlong, presumably because he was a bigger star than James Caan in that country.

A major film production and distribution company, Lionsgate, bought the movie from me and promoted it all over the world through DVD sales and on cable TV. They would have paid me more if the film had a bigger-name director, but that is water under the bridge. It's always a thrill to get calls from people telling me they've seen the movie—and my niece once called me from her hotel room in Chile to tell me it was on TV there.

So what did I get for $5 million? A record of my life—but more importantly, I got my message out into the world and created a legacy for my children and grandchildren. Very few people have the opportunity and the resources to do what I did, and I am thrilled that I took the chance to make a movie of my life.

In the end, I didn't lose any money by making the movie my own way, and it certainly gave me a good education in the way Hollywood works. It was the experience of a lifetime, but I'm not in a hurry to do it again. After the film came out, I was approached by several other producers who wanted me to make movies with them. I considered their offers, but I had accomplished what I'd set out to do, so I turned them down. I made the movie that I wanted to make, and I don't feel the need to make another one, even if it continues my story to bring it up to the present.

CHAPTER 16

KING OF SPRING STREET

The conversion of my first high-rise building at 639 South Spring Street in downtown Los Angeles was a landmark event—it was the first building to take advantage of the Adaptive Reuse Ordinance and the first building that led to the transformation of a beautiful part of Los Angeles. I had waited for many years for something like this to happen, and when it did I was ready to take full advantage of it.

It was an exciting time because I was in the center of the revitalization of what is my favorite neighborhood in Los Angeles. I love everything vintage, from historic buildings to classic cars, and once I realized that the Adaptive Reuse Ordinance was going to have such a positive effect on the neglected downtown area, I started looking around for another project to take on.

As work progressed at 639 South Spring Street in 1999,

the building next door at 621 became available. I managed to buy it in May 2000, and in June 2002, I bought the building at 601 on the corner of South Spring Street and Sixth Street. Each of the buildings I bought on this block is a spectacular historic structure, and at that point I owned most of the block on that side of South Spring Street between Sixth and Seventh Streets.

Fortunately—because of the Adaptive Reuse Ordinance—I did not have to let these newly acquired buildings sit empty for long. I am a property landlord who fixes up his buildings as soon as possible and creates foot traffic again, encouraging pedestrians to walk into sidewalk cafés and well-maintained stores.

When I bought it, 621 had been run and managed very poorly and was in terrible condition. I take great pride in my properties, so I revitalized the building and brought it back to its former glory. It was a desirable property once again, located in a revitalized area, and I brought in good tenants.

People were returning to downtown LA, and you could sense the change in attitude throughout the neighborhood. The air of depression was lifting, and people felt optimistic and hopeful.

The building at 601 was once the Hayward Hotel, a well-known landmark in downtown Los Angeles. The main building had been constructed in 1905, and at eight stories high, it was one of the very first high-rises downtown. A ninth floor was added in 1916 and major additions on the adjoining land were made over the next ten years, including a fourteen-story tower next door. In total, the Hayward Hotel complex had three buildings with 525 rooms and a whole lot of retail space on the ground floor.

Before the Hayward was built, the neighborhood was residential, and across the street there was a Ralphs Brothers Grocery, which developed into one of the largest supermarket chains in Southern California. Until the 1940s, a legendary jazz club, Rhythm Room, whose motto was "Just for Fun," played in the hotel's basement.

After World War II, the downtown area lost businesses to the suburbs and people no longer needed to spend the night in hotels. Then in the 1960s and 1970s, bigger hotels such as the Hilton, Sheraton, and Marriott were built in the new downtown to cater to the influx of new businesses and tourists—but smaller and older hotels like such as Hayward, Alexandria, and Bristol in the old downtown suffered due to high vacancies and were eventually converted to residential apartments.

When I bought it in June 2002, the Hayward Hotel's 525 rooms were being used for low-income housing. It had definitely seen better days. Not long before I bought it, the *Los Angeles Times* described it as "a labyrinth of hallways, staircases and elevators… infested with cockroaches and rodents; the smell of dead rats lingers in the air. The carpeting in today's Hayward is pock-marked with cigarette burns from tenants who prefer the carpet to ashtrays."[1]

---

1 Lorenza Munoz, "Problems Plague City-Backed Hotel: Housing: Drugs, Crime Are Rampant at Downtown Hotel Renovated under Ambitious Program, Police Say. But Officials Say Progress Is Being Made," *Los Angeles Times*, November 25, 1995, https://www.latimes.com/archives/la-xpm-1995-11-25-me-6994-story.html

The previous developer who converted the hotel into affordable housing stole millions of dollars of government money that had been earmarked for the project. He went to prison, and the building went into foreclosure. When the bank put the building up for auction at a foreclosure sale on the courthouse steps, I ended up buying it.

The first things I did when I purchased the building were renovate the courtyard and common area, paint the walls, and make it look respectable again. As soon as I began renovating the Hayward, however, the Los Angeles Community Action Network (LA CAN)—an activist organization for homelessness—started protesting right outside the building. I spoke to the leader of the group, and he told me they were protesting because I was going to kick out everyone who was currently living in the building. I told him that wasn't what I was going to do.

In fact, we fixed the vacant units first, and once those were finished, we moved some of the existing tenants into the nice, clean, refurbished units so we could renovate their old units. Slowly, the building came back to life and most of the tenants— even the low-income and semi-homeless people who were living on government assistance—returned to clean, well-designed, beautiful apartments. Not only was this the opposite of what the protestors had feared, but the tenants literally applauded me for what I'd done to help them.

The next thing I did with the Hayward Hotel was get rid

of the seedy liquor store that was on the street level. The store owners were paying around $6,000 a month in rent, but they were willing to pay me double their rent when I told them I was not renewing the lease. I refused to renew it because the liquor store was bad for the neighborhood and it brought the wrong crowd to the area. Instead, I leased the space to a café with outside seating for a much lower price than the liquor store was paying. It was important to do this because I wanted to make the neighborhood safer, plus it created a much more pleasant vibe for everyone, including the residents.

I was really happy to be able to clean up the building and give the tenants a more comfortable way of life. We brought it back to its original glory and turned it into Hayward Manor Apartments—complete with the iconic "Hotel Hayward" sign running down the corner of the building at South Spring Street and Sixth Street. It still has its original character, but work like that does not come cheap, and I spent millions of dollars on the renovations. I also revived the Rhythm Room, complete with its art nouveau details and fabulous dance floor. A few years later, the building served as the backdrop to the pivotal scene in the 2007 Michael Bay movie *Transformers*, where Megatron and Optimus Prime battle for control.

I also leased out other spaces in my buildings on South Spring Street to restaurants, ice cream parlors, sidewalk cafés, hair salons, and boutiques. The buildings were beautiful and had good reputations for being in a trendy and desirable area, and companies like Starbucks that were aggressively expanding really wanted to open a location in the Hayward. I was thrilled when Starbucks signed a lease there and became one of the anchors of my properties.

Many of the cafés and restaurants included outdoor seating, which gave them a European and cosmopolitan feel. It's essential to have foot traffic around well-maintained buildings in downtown areas, because that conveys a sense of safety and encourages people to spend more time there.

* * *

About a year after I completed the Hayward Hotel renovations, a buyer came to me with an offer to buy the building. The price was so good that I couldn't say no. They asked for a thirty-day contingency before the deal closed, which allowed them to do their due diligence. That was a normal request, so I agreed.

My plan was to take the money from that sale and move on to my next project. The best part was that it would give me a tax break, which would allow me to defer paying taxes on the profit—but only if I reinvested the money in another similar property. I'd done this before, so I knew the rules and assumed I could essentially exchange this building for another one like it.

What I didn't realize was that in the few years since the Adaptive Reuse Ordinance had been passed, the price of real estate had shot up in the historic downtown area. I knew the price of my own properties had skyrocketed because of the improvements I had made to them, but I was shocked to find that everything else had also appreciated quite considerably. There was literally nothing even close to my price range that I could invest in for the exchange, so I was looking at a hefty tax bill if the deal went through. I realized I had made a huge mistake.

As the thirty-day contingency deadline approached, I was praying that the buyers would not remove the contingency. That way, I could turn the deal down and save myself the pain of buying another building that I couldn't afford—or paying a hefty tax bill that wouldn't leave much of the profit in my own hands.

The deadline for the thirty-day contingency was at 5:00 p.m. on the relevant day. At 5:05 p.m., I received an email from the buyers telling me they were neither approving nor disapproving the deal. I considered that to be a disapproval, however, and moved forward with canceling the transaction—and I took the opportunity, as outlined in the original contract, to tell them I was not selling them the property. They were upset and refused to accept the cancellation, and they tried to keep the deal open. Apparently, they really wanted the Hayward, and about a week later I received a letter from their attorney requesting that I keep to the original agreement and sell them the building.

My attorney told me I was well within my rights to stop the sale. However, even though the contract was clear and I had the legal right to do what I did—especially because the investors did not approve or disapprove the sale—my attorney was nervous about going to court because you never know what a jury will do. The fact that the buyers were five minutes past the deadline was a minor technicality, and the jury could just as easily decide to overlook the technicality and force the sale. We went back and forth over this issue for six months, and I spent more than a quarter of a million dollars on attorney's fees. The buyers probably spent the same amount, and we were no closer to an agreement than we were at the start.

At this point, I told my attorney that I had an idea and that I wanted to meet with the buyers—just the buyers, with no attorneys in the room. Both my attorney and their attorney thought this was a bad idea, but the buyers agreed to meet me for lunch, so we scheduled a meeting at a restaurant in Beverly Hills.

As soon as the buyers sat down at the restaurant with me, they jumped straight into talking business and asked me what my idea was. I told them I wouldn't talk business on an empty stomach, so we ordered lunch and some wine, and we discussed other things. I learned they were immigrants from India and, like me, had arrived in the US at a young age.

After we ordered dessert, I told them, "OK, now let's talk business." I started by saying, "I've already spent a quarter of a million dollars in attorney's fees, and I bet you guys have spent as much. How much more are you willing to spend on the case?"

"As much as it takes," they responded.

"Well, let me tell you something," I said. "I am exactly the same way, and I will also spend as much as it takes to win." I told them that my chance of winning was much better than theirs because I had the contract on my side, but it would take each of us another $500,000 in attorney's fees to go to court and get a judgment—and if the judge or jury sided with them, I would appeal it, adding perhaps an additional $250,000 in attorney's fees.

"So here's what I'm proposing," I said. "I'm not selling you the property, but I will hand half a million dollars to you to drop the case. Between this half a million dollars and the half a million dollars you won't need to spend on attorneys and probably lose the case, you're ahead $1 million, and you walk away a winner."

They said no. Then they told me they'd consider an offer, but that it could not be less than $1 million. At that point, I knew they were ready to settle. They wanted a deal, and they were hooked.

This is beautiful, I thought to myself. *We are in the game.*

I told them again that my number was $500,000—and that when I finished my dessert I was leaving, and the offer would leave with me. They said I shouldn't be in a rush to leave and that they would accept $700,000 and not a dollar less. I remained firm at $500,000 and not a dollar more. They said no, repeating that they were firm at $700,000. Neither one of us was budging, and it looked like we had reached an impasse.

"OK," they said. "We're going to keep fighting you."

"Be my guest," I said. "I did my best, but I'm walking away."

When we left the restaurant, we were standing on the sidewalk together waiting to cross the street. I told them, "When the light turns green, we are each walking our own separate ways."

As soon as I finished saying that, the light turned green and I started walking toward my car. That's when one of them said, "How soon can your attorney prepare the settlement agreement for $500,000?"

The next day, we handed them the settlement agreement. The money was transferred, and I walked away from a costly litigation. Overall, this mistake cost me more than $750,000: $500,000 to the would-be buyers and over $250,000 to my attorneys. However, it was worth it in the long run because I was able to save the Hayward once again.

* * *

While this drama was going on with the Hayward, I continued to look for more historic high-rises to renovate in the neighborhood. The opportunity came up to buy a few more in the Historic Core in and around South Spring Street, including 626 South Spring Street, which became City Lofts; 724 South Spring Street, now known as the Corporation Building; and 609 South Grand Avenue, which was turned into Milano Lofts.

South Spring Street used to be the heart of the Los Angeles financial district. Many large banks had their headquarters on the street in imposing high-rises, and the Stock Exchange Building was the headquarters of the Los Angeles Stock Exchange from 1931 to 1986. It was the biggest stock exchange west of the Mississippi River. Built in 1931 in the art deco style, it is one of the most elegant and distinctive buildings in Los Angeles. The bronze front doors are said to be the largest of their kind in the city.

However, the timing of the building's construction was terrible. Ground was broken just days before the devastating stock market crash on October 29, 1929, that marked the start of the Great Depression. By the time the building was completed in 1931, the nation was in the firm grip of the Depression. The imposing granite facade is fifty-three feet high, and the twelve-story office tower behind it was about the maximum height allowed at the time it was built.

By the 1980s, the Los Angeles Stock Exchange had outgrown its space, and in 1986 it moved north to South Beaudry Avenue, nearer the Bunker Hill area that was the new downtown Los Angeles with its towering skyscrapers. Like the other build-ings in the Historic Core, the Stock Exchange Building became vacant and fell into disuse. For a while, it was the site of a night-club that was appropriately called The Stock Exchange, and later it became another well-known nightclub called Exchange LA. It was also used as a place to shoot commercials, television shows, and movies, most notably *The Big Lebowski*, which was released in 1998.

The size of the buildings on South Spring Street meant that I ended up owning most of the 600 block—601, 609, 621, and 639 on the west side and 626 on the east side. I also added the old Alexandria Hotel at 501 South Spring Street in January 2012 and another high-rise at 724 South Spring Street in December 2012. Owning most of the block gave me the ability to maintain that area and to keep it clean and safe for the community.

The eight-story Alexandria Hotel was built in 1906 and was one of the most stylish and refined hotels in downtown Los Angeles. Until the Biltmore Hotel was built in 1923 just a few blocks away, the Alexandria Hotel was renowned as the most luxurious in LA and was always a prized destination for its three gorgeous ballrooms. It was popular with Hollywood movie stars in the 1920s and 1930s. Rudolph Valentino stayed in the penthouse, and it even hosted Charlie Chaplin's wedding.

As with the rest of the old downtown, the Alexandria suffered from neglect in the 1970s and later. Poorly managed, the hotel became a shabby shell of its former self. Just like the Hayward, we fixed it up and brought it back to its original condition, transforming it into a clean and comfortable space where tenants were proud to live. I was happy to give it life again.

I didn't set out to buy a lot of properties on this one stretch of South Spring Street, but opportunities kept coming my way. All of my buildings have been beautifully renovated, and I added thousands of residential units to the area. I also helped to revitalize the Historic Core by creating foot traffic for the street-level businesses that I encouraged to move into the ground floor of my buildings.

At one point, an article ran in a newspaper that called me the "King of Spring Street," a title I appreciated because I felt like it was my responsibility to look after the buildings and to make the street as vibrant as it was in its heyday. The article also gave me credit for doing what the City of Los Angeles had been trying to do for decades but had always failed to achieve—revitalize the old downtown. I am proud that I helped change the dynamic of this neighborhood from an unattractive eyesore that nobody wanted anything to do with to one that was attracting thousands of new residents and hundreds of new businesses.

One of the most memorable people to move into my building was Tony Medina, the first tenant in my first high-rise at 639 South Spring Street. Tony was a line producer in the movie industry, the guy who basically runs everything and makes sure the production runs smoothly. I had known him for several years because he often worked on movies that were shot on my properties. A brilliant guy, Tony was always encouraging me to renovate the old buildings and convert them to lofts and condos. When I started the work at 639 South Spring Street in 1999, he told me he wanted to rent a loft there. Sure enough, he became the first tenant when he leased the top unit on the fourteenth floor. I really liked and respected Tony, and he stayed in that loft until he tragically passed away in 2021.

* * *

While all this was taking place on Spring Street, I was also purchasing other buildings in the neighborhood and in other parts of Los Angeles. But that stretch of South Spring Street gave me a lot of pride because it changed so dramatically and brought a lot of new residents and businesses into the area. It was something like the board game Monopoly, where you buy as many properties in one neighborhood as you can, because that increases the value of all the properties.

When I first became involved in the historic Los Angeles downtown area, you could appreciate the beauty of the buildings, but the retailers at the street level had changed the way the buildings looked. They took away the attractiveness and replaced it with ugly and distasteful storefronts with tacky, rundown 1950s and 1960s decor. The first thing I did to bring back the historic look of the buildings was to find old photographs to reference so I could make the buildings look as close as they could to the way they once looked in their prime.

This is why it was so heartbreaking to see what happened on my street in the spring of 2020 when rioters took over in the aftermath of George Floyd's death at the hands of police officers in Minneapolis. Demonstrations took place all over the US, and unfortunately, some of them became violent. There was a huge demonstration in LA, and because the Los Angeles City Hall is just a few blocks away at 200 North Spring Street, my neighborhood became the center of activity.

On May 30, 2020, things got out of hand and the demonstration became a riot. People smashed storefronts along South Spring Street and other streets in the neighborhood, and they looted the stores. One of the stores that was violently attacked was the Starbucks in my Hayward Hotel building at the corner of South Spring Street and Sixth Street.

From my office, I could look out the window and see the riot developing. It was upsetting to see what was happening to

208

my beloved neighborhood. People were setting buildings on fire, breaking storefront windows, and stealing everything they could carry. A restaurant owner in one of my neighboring buildings had his restaurant destroyed. He lost millions of dollars and was so discouraged that he never reopened the restaurant. The whole experience was frightening and depressing, and it made me question whether I had made the right decision to renovate all these buildings. If the rioters cared so little that they were willing to destroy everything, what was the point of putting so much work into these buildings in the first place?

I was sympathetic to the demonstrators, and I respected the people who were protesting and demanding justice. However, protest is one thing—looting and destroying other people's property is another. It is a disgusting act of violence. The riots and the destruction that followed set us back twenty years to when I'd first started renovating the neighborhood. Fortunately, I am an optimist and I know that things will get better again. We are in the process of bringing the neighborhood back *again* and repairing the damage—and I am continuing to buy properties there. I am fully committed to this neighborhood, and I want to see it come back better and stronger. After all, I *was* named the King of Spring Street!

CHAPTER 17

BENEFIT OF
THE DOUBT

O ne of the hurdles I have to deal with as the owner of a large portfolio, especially in a sprawling city like Los Angeles, is that I inevitably run into roadblocks with the city council and other property developers. Like anyone else in my line of business, I dealt with numerous legal issues over the years—but the more properties you own and the more high-profile you become, the more you have to deal not only with things like planning approvals and zoning regulations but also with every type of neighborhood issue.

I have found that the best way to deal with almost any situation like this is to step back, take a deep breath, and give the other person the credit they are due. I have always preached this to the younger generations, telling them that the formula to success is simple: be a go-getter, be motivated, be honest, be fair, and always give the other person the benefit of the doubt.

Of course, some people will try to take advantage of your kindness, mistaking it for weakness—but you will never be weak if you are fair and honest. Stealing and deception are the easy ways out and are the characteristics of a cowardly and broken person, whereas standing up for your rights and your beliefs often takes courage and determination. I don't always win, but I don't get upset if I am beaten by a better opponent. The last thing I would ever want to be accused of is gaining an unfair advantage through deception or theft.

It all comes down to following the guiding principle of my life: choose the path that will lead to the right decision.

* * *

Back in 1978, when I was nineteen, I bought the old gas station on the corner of West Boulevard and Pico Boulevard for $90,000. It was a struggle to come up with the money, but it allowed me to live out my dream of working with cars and opening my auto bay business. It was my first real estate purchase, and I turned that old gas station into a profitable venture. It was also where my professional life really started to take shape and it was where I met my wife, so it has a deep emotional attachment for me.

I built ten auto bays on that property, and I rented out five of them to an incredible mechanic named Leon. He was paying me $1,500 per month for each auto bay for a total of $7,500 a month. He was making good money, and I was happy with the arrangement. It was going so well that Leon wanted to expand, and he would have rented out the rest of the auto bays if they had been available.

One day, after he'd been renting from me for more than ten years, Leon came to me and said, "Izek, I've been your tenant for all these years, and now I want to own my own property. You've had this business for a long time, but would you sell it to me?"

I had never even thought about selling the property. It gave me a good income and the freedom to move into the tract home business without taking too much risk. I also didn't want to sell it because it held such sentimental value for me, but I could see Leon's point, and I realized it could be a win-win situation for both of us: Leon would own his own business and I could take the money and invest it in another project. After I thought about it some more and discussed it with Aline, I told Leon I would sell him the property. He offered me $750,000 and I agreed, on the condition that we would close the deal in three months. We didn't have a written agreement, but we trusted each other to do the right thing.

Leon was thrilled, and he went to work right away to find the financing. I thought $750,000 was a fair price. I had paid $90,000 for the property, but that was about fifteen years earlier, and I'd invested about $200,000 in improvements. The rental income alone justified the price.

Three months went by and I didn't hear anything from Leon about the purchase, so I assumed he hadn't been able to raise the money. To be honest, I was a little relieved, because I'd started to regret the idea of selling the property because of its sentimental value. Another six months went by, and that's when Leon came to my office and told me he'd managed to raise the $750,000.

"That's great," I told him, "but where have you been for the past six months? The agreement was for three months. You missed the deadline, and I really don't want to sell it now."

"Please don't do this to me," he said. "I've been working hard. This is my dream, and I've been planning what I'd do with it. I never thought it would be possible, but you were making it possible for me. Don't take it away from me now."

"I'm sorry," I said, "but you missed the deadline."

"But I've already spent $20,000 to get the loan and an appraisal," he said. I could see the sadness in his eyes. "I've wasted all that money."

"Look," I said, "I understand your frustration, and I am not going to let you take a $20,000 loss. Even though it's not my fault, I will cover the $20,000 for you so you won't suffer any losses, but I'm not willing to sell it now."

As we sat there in silence, I realized I was standing in this guy's way. What if people had treated me like this back when I was getting started? Where would I be today? Leon was doing the exact same thing I had done fifteen years earlier—chasing his dream and following his heart. How could I deny him his dream when so many people had helped me and shown me the way forward?

"You know what?" I told him. "I've enjoyed this property

214

for fifteen years, but it's time for a change. God bless you; we can proceed with the sale."

I sold Leon the property for $750,000, and he went on to become a successful business owner and landlord. I'm glad I sold it to him, but that old gas station still has an emotional attachment for me, and I would buy it back today at virtually any price.

*　*　*

In my business ventures, I almost always worked alone, but there was one partner I trusted enough to work with. He was a very successful businessman and real estate investor in Los Angeles. We worked together on several major projects in the historic downtown, including the purchase of three notable hotels in 2012.

Each of us brought different skills and perspectives to the table, and we had a good working relationship. When I was negotiating to purchase a property on the 400 block of South Spring Street, the property value was around $40 million. I had the opportunity to get it at a very good deal due to the fact that the owner was in distress and was going to lose the property to the bank. I discovered I could buy the building from him for only half of what it was worth. It was a rare opportunity and I did not want to miss it. The issue was that I did not have all the money available at that moment. I had just finished building twenty-five townhomes in Beverly Hills, and most of my liquidity was tied up in that project for the next three months. I needed $20 million immediately.

So I went to my partner and offered him a 50 percent partnership in this purchase, with a potential quick $20 million to be made as profit. "I'm willing to share the profit with you," I told him, "but on the condition that you will front the $20 million for a period of three months." This was too good a deal to turn down, so he immediately agreed.

Unfortunately, the agreement was verbal and nothing was put in writing, although I did have an email in which we discussed the building and the partnership. On the day of closing escrow, he came to me and said, "Izek, I'm not going to invest $20 million for three months with a 50 percent partnership. I'm only willing to give you 20 percent."

I told him absolutely not—I would not let him cut me down to 20 percent. "You can't drag it to the last day of closing and put me in this situation," I said. He was unconcerned and replied, "Take it or not. It is what it is. Either you get 20 percent or nothing."

"What you are doing is wrong," I said, "and I am not going to tolerate it. I've never sued anyone in more than thirty years in business, and please don't let yourself be the first." He ignored me, though, and purchased the property by himself, so I had no option but to sue him.

That was such a disappointing outcome. Up to then, I had no idea that my partner could act this way. I had been in the same room with him when he had given millions of dollars to charities, and I never imagined he would turn around and try to screw me.

Before we went to trial, I reached out and explained to my partner how, in effect, he was stealing from me. I literally showed him everything I would use in court, including the email, and I sent him letters and talked to him over and over again. I told him I wasn't going to let him get away with it, but he wouldn't listen to reason. He was like the schoolyard bully who dared me to stand up to him—and I think he was a little shocked when I did.

"I've shown you all the facts, and I know that a judge and jury will see it my way," I told him. "It's all there in black and white, but I'll give you the benefit of the doubt and offer you a way out."

I went on to tell him that there was a potential profit of $20 million to be made from the disputed property. "Here's what I propose," I said. "The $20 million profit will go to neither of us. One hundred percent of it will be donated to a charity." In addition, I told him the three other properties we owned as partners had a potential for a $25 million profit and that we should sell them and give all the profits to charity. "It all goes to charity," I said, "so nobody ends up ahead. You won't have a guilty verdict on your record, and you won't feel defeated. In fact, you'll feel like a hero for giving millions of dollars to charity."

He didn't even have the courtesy to respond to my offer, and so we went to trial. My lawsuit specifically stated that he had defrauded me, and that was the issue my attorney pressed throughout the trial. The trial lasted for over a month, but in the end all twelve jurors found my partner—now my *former* partner*—guilty of fraud, and he had to pay me punitive damages of millions of dollars, just like I had warned him. It was very sad to see someone lose like that. His dishonest tactics were exposed, and it gave me a good feeling to prove that I was right and that he was wrong. It showed me yet again that you can't expect to get ahead through cheating and fraud, and I was hoping it would be a lesson to him as well. Unfortunately, he did not learn from it.

My former partner's behavior is not all that unusual in the business world. I've seen it a lot, when bad people try to cover up their shameless acts with a good public relations team. It's like the individual has a split personality, where they make sure they're seen giving a lot of money to charities and supporting high-profile civic causes, but at the same time they are cheating and swindling in private.

To me, this is the worst type of person, and I can honestly say that I have never fallen into this trap. The person you see in public is the same person you see in private. I would never do what my former partner did, and I have never knowingly gone into business ventures with people like that. We learn from our mistakes, and in this unfortunate case, I learned that not everyone—even the people you think you know well—should be trusted.

My former partner's loss in court probably made little financial difference to him. He was so rich that he wouldn't even notice the millions of dollars he handed over to me, but I can only imagine how empty he must have felt inside. There are several Old Testament sayings that a wealthy person who covets his money is the only one who will never be satisfied with himself. That means you should never be greedy and take advantage of others. My former partner failed on both counts, and he did not learn his lesson.

About five years after I won my case, I got a call from another real estate developer in Los Angeles. "I heard that your partner cheated you and that you sued him and won millions of dollars," he said. The settlement was supposed to be confidential, but apparently word had gotten around. I told the real estate developer that I couldn't talk about it, but then he dropped the bombshell: "What happened to you is the exact same thing he's doing to me right now."

The guy who called me was a kind and trusting person whom I admired. We served together on the board of a major charity in Los Angeles, and he was a true gentleman both in public and in private. He explained to me that he had found a piece of property for $3.5 million in the exclusive Hidden Hills gated community in Los Angeles, which was home to a lot of celebrities and sports stars, but he didn't have the cash on hand to make the purchase. My former partner agreed to partner with him and showed him how they could turn the property around and make as much as a $5 million profit. The agreement was that my former partner would put up the money and they would develop the property and share the profit equally—but just like with me, the partner was careful to make sure there was nothing in writing.

A week before the deal was supposed to be closed, the partner called my friend and told him he was going to buy the property but that he was going to give him only 20 percent instead of the 50 percent they had agreed on—exactly the same thing he had done to me. When my friend said that 20 percent wasn't the deal, the partner told him, "Well, you can buy it yourself, but how are you going to do that? What are you going to do about it?"

My friend was very upset that the partner was trying to take advantage of him, and he vowed to bring in another investor to put up all the money and shut out the partner. He wasn't calling me to go in on the deal with him, but I was so mad that my former partner was still trying to bully and cheat people even after I'd exposed his lies and crooked ways that I told my friend I would put up the money and he could do the construction. I knew this would make my former partner steaming mad!

To make a long story short, we bought the property and built a fifteen-thousand-square-foot mansion on it. We sold it to a huge sports star and made a good profit, and I honored my agreement. It was all legit, and not a penny went to my former partner.

* * *

In all my years in the United States, starting in 1973 when I first arrived in Los Angeles, I never felt discriminated against because I was a foreigner. That's one of the things I love about the US—you are judged by the quality of your work and, as

Martin Luther King Jr. hoped for, the content of your character. If you work hard and do good, honest work, you can succeed.

The closest I came to feeling discriminated against was when I was going through the process of buying my second high-rise at 621 South Spring Street in early 2000. It was the first time in my life that I felt attacked because I was a foreigner, but in the end it proved to be a misunderstanding and not xenophobia.

The high-rise at 621 South Spring Street was significant to the history of Los Angeles. It was built in the historic downtown in 1930, but by the early 1980s the neighborhood had become derelict when businesses moved to the new downtown at Bunker Hill. Like everything else around it, 621 South Spring Street became vacant. A developer, together with the Community Redevelopment Agency (CRA)—part of the City of Los Angeles Housing Department—bought 621 South Spring Street with the idea of turning it into housing. They converted it into one hundred and twenty condominiums.

This was a one-off development, with no real plan to revitalize the more extensive historic downtown. Still, over the next ten years or so, people bought the condos in the hope that the city would deal with the homelessness that was overrunning the area and would revive the historic downtown so that businesses and residents could return to it.

By the mid-1990s, though, nothing was happening. The only occupied building in that part of the historic downtown was 621 South Spring Street. The owners felt betrayed, and they sued the CRA, claiming they had bought the condos with the understanding that the CRA would return the historic down-town to its original glory. Instead, things were actually getting worse and people didn't feel safe leaving the building after dark.

The residents wanted out, so the CRA started buying the condos back. Meanwhile, the developer lost everything in some bad investments. He disappeared, so the CRA ended up taking over the entire project. By 1999, the CRA owned all the units and was soliciting proposals for what to do next.

The problem was that even though the CRA wanted to get rid of the building and was eager to sell it to me, it was listed as government property, so they had to put it on the open market and let the public bid on it in what is known as a request for proposal. That was fair, so I put in my sealed bid. Other developers put in their sealed bids as well—and when the bids were opened, mine was the highest. Jona Goldrich, a Holocaust survivor who had become a well-known billionaire property developer who built impressive skyscrapers, bid less than I did. All the other bids were between Jona's low bid and my high bid. I was a happy guy because I was the highest bidder, and I knew I was buying the building at a significant discount from its true value. I was excited to get the renovation started.

When you are awarded a city-owned property through this type of auction, you still need to go to the Los Angeles City Council for approval. The city council needed only a majority of its fifteen members to approve the sale. The approval should have been automatic and the completion of the deal should have been a formality. I submitted all the necessary paperwork and attended the city council meeting where they discussed the building, but one particular council member, Nate Holden, objected: "How can we sell a building that cost the city millions of dollars to that young Israeli guy for such a big loss?" He called me "that young Israeli guy" because I was barely forty years old and was pretty much unknown to the city council members outside of my Adaptive Reuse application. I didn't blame him for not wanting to sell the building at such a huge loss.

I got hold of all the bids from the other developers, and my attorney and I went to every one of the city council members to show them that I had won the auction impartially and legally—and to make it clear that I would sue the city if they didn't approve the sale. I talked to all the city council members except Nate Holden, who wouldn't meet with me, and they told me to show my documentation to Nate. I tried doing this, but he still refused to meet with me in his office and I was therefore unable to present my argument. To appease Nate, the city council agreed to an investigation and to put the sale on hold for thirty days.

In one city council meeting—where Nate could not avoid me—I told him that even Jona Goldrich had bid less than me, and Jona knew the value of property in Los Angeles better than anyone. If anything, I was overpaying.

Nate's response floored me: "Maybe there's some monkey business going on. I know Jona is an older Israeli guy, and maybe he's paving the road ahead for a new, younger Israeli guy."

Again, Nate appeared to be accusing me of being the "young Israeli guy" who was trying to get something for nothing. My bid was legitimate, and so was Jona's. To be clear, I knew who Jona Goldrich was, but I'd never met him in my life. The accusation was outrageous and the most unfair thing that anyone has ever said to me. But Nate's opposition looked like it was going to kill the deal and I would lose out on the building.

For over a week, Nate continued to ignore my calls. We were running out of time and the thirty-day period was about to expire, so Aline and I made one last effort to try to reach Nate. As we were riding in the elevator at the LA City Hall after another failed attempt to see him, it stopped, and Nate's private secretary walked in. She already knew us, so Aline reached out to her and asked for her help in arranging a meeting. The secretary told Aline she would do what she could.

Still feeling discouraged, we drove home assuming that the deal was never going to happen. Just minutes after we got home, however, the phone rang. It was Nate's private secretary. "Get over here now," she said. "Nate will be in his office in thirty minutes, and he is ready to meet you." We jumped back in the car and raced over to Nate's office.

On my way there, I called my attorney, and he advised me that it was not a good idea to meet with Nate, but if I did he wanted to be present. I told him that we were going in a friendly, not legal, way to present my argument and that there was no need for him to come.

When we arrived at Nate's office, Nate looked at me and gave me a smile. "By the comment I made, it seems like I do not like Israelis," he said.

I smiled and replied, "That's what it felt like."

"Let me show you something," he said, and he led us into another office. The walls were filled with pictures of Israel, and he told me how much he loved Israel and Israelis. I was shocked but things still didn't make sense. I told Nate that I had no relationship with Jona, and he reassured me that it was all going to be OK.

Two days later, the city council voted on the bid. Nate was the only one of the fifteen council members who didn't show up for the vote, and it was passed unanimously. After the vote Nate walked into the city council chambers. I wanted to go and give him a big hug, but he just smiled and gave me a thumbs-up.

Afterward, he told me he didn't want to come in before the vote and look like a fool by voting for the sale when he'd opposed it before. He'd evidently told the other city council members he was OK with the sale and that he no longer had any objections. To be fair to him, he changed his mind when he saw the facts and realized his objections had been a mistake and a misunderstanding.

The weird thing is that even though I had my doubts about Nate due to his unfounded comments, I really don't think he meant them. After meeting with him and proving that I had won the auction fair and square, I realized he did not have an ounce of hate or discrimination in him. He proved to be a true gentleman. I was finally able to buy the building and set to work turning it into a gem.

CHAPTER 18

LIFE REBUILDING CENTER

Homelessness has been an issue in Los Angeles almost since the day the city was founded in the mid-1800s, and obviously there are no easy solutions. I have been particularly aware of the problem ever since I opened my first burger joint on the corner of South Los Angeles Street and East Pico Boulevard in 1975 when I was just sixteen years old. Over the years, I have seen many different attempts to deal with the issue of homelessness, but none of them have worked. In my opinion, they've all just been Band-Aids applied by politicians to make everything look good for a short while. And instead of wondering why the Band-Aid didn't work, they just added more Band-Aids.

Often, the approach to the homeless has been heavy-handed. In 1947, the Los Angeles Police Department claimed that 50 percent of crime in Los Angeles originated in the Skid Row area, the neighborhood near the historic downtown. They arrested more than 350 homeless people, but this draconian measure made no difference and served only to demonize those who were powerless and easy targets.

A city-sponsored "rehabilitation" of Skid Row in the 1950s and 1960s resulted in the demolition of what were known as "nuisance" buildings where the homeless were known to congregate. The problem here was that many of the buildings were low-rent housing options and cheap boardinghouses—so instead of at-risk people having a roof over their heads, they were forced out onto the streets, making the problem even worse and more visible.

There have been many attempts to solve the issue of homelessness over the years, but they generally followed the trend of these failed "social experiments"—rounding up and intimidating the homeless or forcing them to move somewhere else and hoping the problem would disappear with them. After all, it is easier to make something someone else's problem than it is to enact a humane and sensible solution that might make a long-term difference.

From a very young age, I've been a guy who cares about people. I have always had great compassion for my fellow humans, and I always hated to think that my actions would allow people to suffer. There was almost no homelessness in Israel when I was a kid, so seeing the homeless in Los Angeles was a shock to me. Decades later, I still saw the homeless every day as I drove around Los Angeles. One thing that I never did, however, was give them cash directly, because that was not helping them. In fact, it could even make things worse. Most homeless people are in desperate situations, so they will more than likely use the money to buy drugs or alcohol.

Instead of giving the homeless money, I tried to help them in other ways. I believed in educating them and doing all I could to bring them back to a normal life and get their dignity back.

The average rent in Los Angeles in 2022 was more than $2,000 a month for a studio or small apartment, and more for larger apartments and lofts. People want to live in nice areas like the historic downtown district, but there are some really great places in the suburbs as well. However, over $2,500 a month for a place on Spring Street in one of my nicest buildings is a bit too much for many people, especially those who work in the service sector and make not much more than minimum wage. On the other hand, having buildings they aspire to live in is an incentive to work harder so that they might one day be able to move into a better area.

One of the criticisms of high rent is that it is a major contributor to homelessness. I disagree with this theory, because from my own experiences in observing the homelessness crisis through the years, I believe it is caused almost completely by mental health issues and by drug and alcohol addiction and abuse. However, I am very sensitive to the issue of high rents. Out of my own portfolio, which includes many luxury apartments, I have designated about one thousand units to be set aside for low-income and affordable housing, including about a hundred units that I turned over to a city-sponsored charity,

Brilliant Corners, that finds homeless people on the streets and provides housing for them.

Many people cannot afford luxury apartments, even though they work hard and try to do everything right. They could move to the suburbs and find cheaper housing, but many people do not like the suburban lifestyle and would prefer to live in the middle of the city or in the downtown area. I want to help people live out their dreams, which is why I am willing to make housing available for less than the market rate.

I know I could make more money and face fewer problems and deal with less red tape by turning a blind eye to the poor and homeless, but not everything in life is about making money. It's about being thankful for what I've got and giving back to the city and country I love—while at the same time giving people hope and keeping them off the streets. My small contribution means I know there are more than a thousand families who are now a little better off and who have more optimism for the future because I gave them some assistance with their housing.

Still, I often wondered if I could make a bigger difference if I took a more radical approach. What if I could not only provide housing for the homeless and those in danger of becoming homeless but also give them everything that could set them on the path to becoming productive members of society again— from job training and transportation to affordable medical care and childcare?

More importantly, *how* could I do that, and how could I do it at a cost that was competitive with what the city of Los

Angeles was already spending on the failed Band-Aid approach?

*   *   *

I live in the most beautiful country in the world, the United States of America, and in one of the greatest cities, Los Angeles, with its movie stars, famous singers, fancy cars, high-rises with fabulous condominiums, and skyscrapers with powerful businesses and spectacular offices headquartered in them. There's luxury and money everywhere you look, but if you go another block or turn the corner, you'll find what looks like a Third World country. I saw this poverty and homelessness on a daily basis, and before too long I had to ask myself, *How can anyone see this and not do something about it?*

If you don't live in or visit Los Angeles, it can be hard to fathom the extent of the homeless issue. Most cities have a homeless population, but it's nothing compared to the situation in LA. The homeless in New York City are a problem, but it's rare to see more than one or two homeless people in any setting. In Los Angeles, there are many places where you can easily come across dozens or even hundreds of homeless people who dominate the area for blocks on end. To make matters worse, the year-round mild weather attracts a lot of homeless people to LA who come from other cities and states.

As you drive around the city, it's impossible to ignore the increasing number of people living on the streets of Los Angeles. In some parts of the city, sidewalks and other areas by the side of the road are filled with rows of makeshift tents and shelters made out of anything that can provide protection from the elements. There are many places where tents and other shelters have literally taken over the entire sidewalk, so pedestrians have to walk in the street—but the city has made it virtually illegal for the police to break up these "tent cities" or to help the homeless in any meaningful way. The problem is getting worse.

Like most other Angelenos, I thought the city was not doing enough to address the homeless issue—and I was not the only business owner who was concerned that the homeless were deterring people from patronizing our businesses. If the sidewalk in front of your building is blocked by the homeless living in tents, who wants to rent an apartment there or fight their way through to visit a retail store or restaurant?

I know most of these people living on the streets do not want to be there, and I have great sympathy for anyone who is homeless and in such a predicament. They want to live normal lives again, and we should do everything in our power to make that possible—but it is not our responsibility to coddle them; it's our job only to provide the help they need and to assist them on the path to recovery.

The people who understand that they must assume their own responsibility instead of blaming others for their failures are the ones who can successfully make the transition out of homelessness. There are countless examples of people who were once homeless but who, with a little help, became go-getters and built their lives back from nothing.

The other part of the equation is that it is the responsibility of the city and county of Los Angeles to maintain a safe and healthy environment for everyone within their borders—whether they are housed or not. Clearly, the city and county had failed spectacularly on the homelessness issue.

In 2019, I was fed up with seeing the way Los Angeles was deteriorating. The homeless were not only downtown but all over the city. Something had to be done, so I went to the mayor at the time, Eric Garcetti, and explained my frustrations to him. I told him that dealing with the homeless was the city's responsibility, and I suggested ways that the city could solve the homelessness issue.

Garcetti and his team looked at me and told me that they had no answers. I told them, "You are leaving me no other option than to file a lawsuit against the city to make you deal with the homeless." They did not reject this idea; in fact, they almost encouraged me to do it because it would force the city and county to take action in an area where they had no plan or leadership from the city council or the County Board of Supervisors.

As a result of that conversation, I decided to go forward with the lawsuit. I interviewed several attorneys who had the right experience, and I ended up hiring Elizabeth Mitchell and her firm. With the help of a few other property owners, we raised hundreds of thousands of dollars to back the lawsuit. Rather than making it a personal issue, we formed the LA Alliance for Human Rights, which drew up the lawsuit asking the city and county to take responsibility for the homeless and to return the sidewalks to their intended use.

In March 2020, the LA Alliance for Human Rights filed the lawsuit against the city and county of Los Angeles. As outlined on the LA Alliance website, we were seeking:

> A legally enforceable mandate whereby the community provides beds and services to those ready, willing, and able to accept shelter. At the same time, living in public spaces is forbidden and laws are enforced. This is a balanced social contract whereby the community is able to provide for those most vulnerable on our streets while also removing those who exist to prey on those vulnerable and the communities in which they reside.[1]

The lawsuit came before US District Judge David Carter. Just days later, the COVID-19 pandemic shut down everything, including the courthouse, and we received word that the hearing was going to be postponed. Since it was an emergency situation, though, Judge Carter agreed to continue with the lawsuit. I offered to host the hearing at the huge ballroom in the Alexandria Hotel at 501 South Spring Street. The hearing drew some of the most important people in the city, including the mayor, the County Board of Supervisors, members of the city council, the city and county attorneys, and members of

1 "Get the Facts," LA Alliance for Human Rights, https://www.la-alliance.org/get_the_facts.

the media, such as reporters from the *Los Angeles Times* and local television stations. Everyone had to sit at least six feet apart in order for the hearings to be held safely. With pandemic safety precautions in place—including social distancing and masking—the hearings continued for months until the court was able to reopen in its own space.

During this time, I met with Judge Carter, and he told me of a similar lawsuit in Orange County—the county south of Los Angeles County—that he also had presided over. That lawsuit had been settled a few years earlier, and the result was that Orange County was now taking a more humane approach to homelessness. The guy who initiated the lawsuit, Bill Taormina, was a businessman who was in a similar situation to me, but it was on a much smaller scale because the problem there was not as widespread. Judge Carter encouraged me to contact Bill and to see for myself what he had done for the homeless, so I made arrangements to meet Bill in Anaheim.

Bill's approach to the homeless issue blew my mind. He not only had instigated the lawsuit but had come up with a solution to care for the homeless: the Life Rebuilding Center for the homeless. He provided 150 beds for homeless people, along with professional services such as social workers, medical care, a rehab center for those dealing with drug and alcohol addiction, a dental office, a hair salon, and job training.

When I walked through the facility with Bill and my sons Jonathan and Jimmy, the homeless people who were there getting help continuously thanked Bill for what he had done for them. By the time they "graduated" from the center, they would have jobs and homes and would be much better prepared to enter back into society, just like hundreds of others who had passed through the facility before them.

What Bill did in Anaheim was phenomenal, and it didn't take me long to realize that this was also the solution to the homeless problem in Los Angeles. It would not be easy, in part because the homeless situation in LA was at least ten times bigger than the one in Anaheim, which meant we would need a much larger facility, but it seemed that this was the best way to make sure people got the help they needed.

* * *

A few years earlier, in November 2013, I bought the Sears Building, a 1.8-million-square-foot building on twenty-four acres at 2650 East Olympic Boulevard in the Boyle Heights neighborhood of Los Angeles. Olympic and world champion boxer Oscar De La Hoya was originally negotiating to buy the building, but that deal fell through, and I was able to step in and get it for less than half of what De La Hoya had been willing to pay.

The Sears Building sits approximately a mile and a half east of downtown LA. It was constructed with reinforced concrete and completed in 1927 in the art deco style and, at nine stories high with an even taller central tower, it is one of the most iconic buildings in LA. It is also one of the largest reinforced concrete buildings west of the Mississippi River and one of the largest historic buildings of any kind in Los Angeles.

From its opening in 1927 until 1991, the building was used as the Sears mail-order distribution center for the western United States, and located on the ground floor was one of the largest and most successful Sears stores in the nation. It was such a remarkable building that it attracted more than one hundred thousand visitors in its first month of operation, in addition to the thousands who came to shop at the Sears retail store—and it was so large that the Sears employees who were filling mail orders moved around the sprawling facility on roller skates. It was the Amazon of its time. The building is a Los Angeles Historic-Cultural Monument and is listed in the National Register of Historic Places.

My original plan for the Sears Building was to create 1,030 residential units along with 200,000 square feet of creative office space and 100,000 square feet of retail space. The top of the tower would become penthouses, and other parts would become restaurants, outdoor pools, basketball courts, gyms, and every other amenity the residents could imagine. The undeveloped area around the building would be transformed into a park surrounded by boutiques, restaurants, and an "artisanal" café in an old railcar.

This project was so large that it was like developing an entire neighborhood from scratch. Neighborhoods in Los Angeles all have names, so I started calling it the Mail Order District in honor of its original purpose.

After years of going through the planning process,

reviewing architectural designs, dealing with engineering studies and entitlements, pulling the city permits, and so many other things—which together cost millions of dollars—we were ready to start construction.

That was when I first visited Bill in Anaheim. Suddenly, after this life-changing visit, I had a new vision for the old Sears Building and changed my mind about the plan for the Mail Order District. What if, instead of converting the building into condominiums and numerous income-producing retail spaces, I devoted it entirely to a brand-new facility for the homeless? It was a potential solution for homelessness—and a major one at that.

*   *   *

We were supposed to start construction on the Sears Building right before COVID-19 shut everything down in early 2020. Like everyone else, we put our project on hold, and it became the perfect time to reassess my plans for the whole Mail Order District proposal.

I realized that the goals of the LA Alliance lawsuit and my own new plan to convert the Sears Building into something revolutionary for the homeless were intersecting. My new focus was on developing a homeless center like the one Bill Taormina was running in Anaheim, but much larger. The new development at the Sears Building became known as the LA Life Rebuilding Center, and I decided I would fund the development myself.

Instead of building 1,030 condos of various sizes for

long-term residents, my new plan was to provide somewhere between 2,500 to 5,000 private beds in private cubicle spaces that would be used only for a short period of time, perhaps no more than six months, while the homeless person or family got the attention, help, and rehabilitation they needed. With job training, medical care, a pharmacy, a hair salon and barbershop, three meals a day, and help finding employment all under one roof, the residents could become rehabilitated. They could then move out and start renting their own apartments, freeing up the units for the next batch of residents. Every person who succeeded would no longer be dependent on the government.

My proposal for the Life Rebuilding Center would be nowhere near as profitable as my first idea for the Mail Order District. To me, it did not make a difference, because people living on the streets need to be rehabilitated and get their dignity back. It was time to give back to the community and make an effort to save humankind.

While I was happy to front the money to get the Life Rebuilding Center up and running, the city and county would still be technically responsible for the cost of running the operation. Everything would be centralized, making it easy for everyone to give and receive help, and a host of charities and homeless organizations like the Salvation Army and the Be Well Foundation were on board and committed to providing services.

Like many other projects in life, the Life Rebuilding Center could work because of the economies of scale and being concentrated in one location instead of spread throughout dozens of locations across the city. Officially, there were over 66,000 homeless people in the city and county of Los Angeles when I was developing this plan, but most homeless shelters had between 100 to 1,000 beds. And that was basically all they offered—a bed and possibly a meal. Then it was back out on the streets with no medical care, no treatment for mental health issues, no facilities for drug rehabilitation, and no training for a potential job.

In other words, what the city offered was the Band-Aid approach in which the standard homeless shelter does not help the homeless person and offers no long-term solutions. It's no good just giving people a bed or even an apartment, because without the support network of social care, medical care, drug rehabilitation, job training, and learning new life skills, there's more than a good chance they will end up right back on the streets.

What the Life Rebuilding Center offered was hope, dignity, and a chance to succeed. It wouldn't replace the other shelters, but it would be an alternative and a model for the future. Over a five- or ten-year period, we could make meaningful inroads into the homeless problem. There will always be homeless people, but our infrastructure would put a massive dent in the problem.

I estimated that the Life Rebuilding Center could provide a place to live and all the services and support for rehabilitation for about $90 to $100 per person per day, with the expectation that a great number of residents would never return to

Me at the age of four wearing
my Halloween costume, 1963.

Sitting on the balcony of my house, 1972.

My parents, Hannan and Sara, in Tel Aviv preparing their move to Los Angeles, 1974.

Jacob and Abe in Jacob's casino
a couple of months before
shutting it down, 1972.

My brother, Abe (left), and
my cousin, Levi (right), 1967.

David Berger→

Abe→

Me→

Me with some of Abe's friends. This was one
month before the 1972 Munich Olympics
and we are on a Tel Aviv Beach.

Me in my body shop's office, 1978.

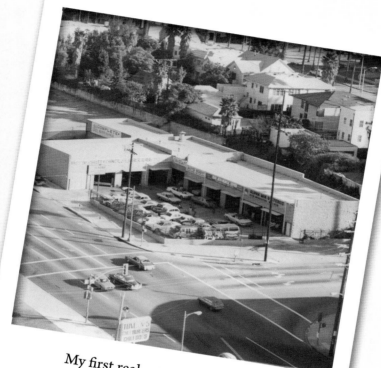

My first real estate development,
the auto bays, 1981.

Double dating with Yoni and his wife, 1982.

The first week of dating Aline.
Visiting the Queen Mary
in Long Beach, CA, 1980.

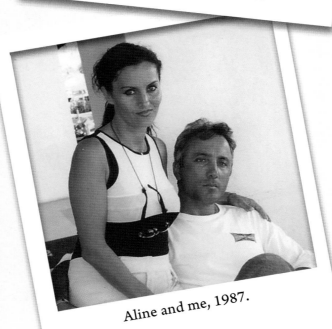

Aline and me, 1987.

Aline and me at the premiere
for my movie, 2012.

My family and I are at the premiere
for our movie, 2012.

The grand opening of one of my projects in Los Angeles, 2020.

The grand opening of one of my projects in Los Angeles, 2020.

Aline and me, 2023.

Jacob, Abe, Aline, and Izek at The Shomof
50 Years Celebration in America, 2023.

My family, 2020.

My two sons, Jonathan and Jimmy, and I
are on the roof of one of our development projects
in Los Angeles, 2015.

Speaking to the media about solving homelessness by developing the Life Rebuilding Center in the Sears Building, 2022.

The first high-rise I purchased in Los Angeles.
It was the first adaptive- reuse project I completed
and consisted of live-work space, 1991.

The Sears Building, 2023.

Top right: Fourteen-year-old me
visiting a local winery, 1973.

Main Photo: Fifty years later,
me in my home wine cellar, 2023.

homelessness. The city already paid this amount or more just to shelter homeless people, without providing anything else. I was offering the building and the buildout at no cost to the city, so their overall expenses to house the homeless would be about the same but the results would be dramatically different in the long run.

I saw that as a slam-dunk just on the costs alone—but when I added in all the extra benefits, it seemed impossible to come up with any objections. After all, for the same amount the city was already spending on the issue of homelessness, the Life Rebuilding Center would give them much better results and they would reap all the benefits—fewer homeless people, a more productive population, and happier constituents.

I remember thinking around that time, *This is a near-perfect deal—a win for me, a win for the city, and most importantly, a win for the homeless people of Los Angeles. What could go wrong?*

I didn't have to wait long to receive an answer to that question.

CHAPTER 19

THE ROAD AHEAD

E ven though the concept of the Life Rebuilding Center was pretty well established, it still needed approval from the Los Angeles City Council and the Board of Supervisors since they would be the ones funding the operation once it was established. Without their consent, there would be no facility. I was committed to paying however much it took to retrofit the Sears Building and to let the city use it. But due to the massive scale of the project, the operational cost was something only the city and county of Los Angeles was capable of funding on a permanent basis.

By early 2021, I had teamed up with Bill Taormina to pitch the Life Rebuilding Center to the city council. Bill was fully on board with the proposal. After working for so long with homeless issues in Orange County, he had built valuable relationships with homeless nonprofits and had put together a coalition to oversee the day-to-day operations at the Life Rebuilding Center in Los Angeles. He fully understood—and supported—what I was trying to do.

The plan was that I would provide the space and do the buildout of the overall operation at a projected cost of about $400 million. The city and county would lease the building from me for a minimum of twenty years, and they would be responsible for the day-to-day operations. Various charities and other providers had already committed to the project and were willing to provide their services.

It was a huge contrast to my original plan for development, which was that I would make a significant profit by converting the building to luxury residential units, creative office space, and retail space. Instead, I was proposing that the city and the county would lease the building from me for the purpose of operating the Life Rebuilding Center to rehabilitate the homeless. As I stated in the previous chapter, in my opinion, a homeless person needs not only housing but also rehabilitation. Simply putting a mentally ill or addicted person in a shelter or home without offering rehabilitation services will find that homeless individual right back on the street again.

The city and county had already spent a massive amount of money to care for the homeless, but it did not provide the benefits the Life Rebuilding Center promised. To be successful in solving the issue, the city just needed to redirect their money to a facility like the Life Rebuilding Center that offered the homeless an opportunity to rehabilitate and that, over the years, would alleviate the city of its overwhelming homelessness problem.

One of the city's solutions to homelessness was building new apartments to house the homeless. However, the city controller in 2020 estimated that the cost of building just one housing unit for one homeless person was about $531,000. We were offering to house the homeless for just a fraction of that cost, plus the Life Rebuilding Center would take care of rehabilitation, health care, and so much more.

Together, Bill and I spoke to all fifteen Los Angeles City Council members, and they all loved the idea—but on major projects like this, they had an unwritten rule that they would essentially defer to the city council member in whose district the project was located.

For the Life Rebuilding Center, this was Kevin de León, who represented the Fourteenth District. Kevin was an experienced Democratic politician who spent almost fourteen years in the California State Assembly and State Senate before being elected to the city council in 2020. He also had near-celebrity status after narrowly losing to Diane Feinstein in the 2018 US Senate election in California.

Kevin was initially very much in favor of my idea for the Life Rebuilding Center. He understood the benefits and advantages of the program, and he even released a statement: "I welcome people who want to productively work on solving this humanitarian crisis and house people as quickly as possible. This is a gargantuan problem that requires all hands on deck to solve, so I am open to all solutions that can address the suffering we see with homelessness."[1]

At the same time, word of the Life Rebuilding Center got out into the community. It was certainly no secret, and we were not trying to hide anything. The *Los Angeles Times* and other newspapers ran stories about our proposal and there were numerous television reports on it. Community groups started to mobilize both to support it and to oppose it. We even created a website to provide information at https://www.liferebuild-ingcenter.com.

In February 2022, Bill and I met with *Los Angeles Times* columnist Gustavo Arellano at the Sears Building. Gustavo was not convinced of the viability of the project when he arrived, but by the time he left he seemed sold on the idea and even wrote a lengthy article in which he called the Life Rebuilding Center "one of the most audacious civic projects I've ever heard of."[2]

While we were giving Gustavo a tour of the Sears Building and showing him what we planned to do, we took him to the top of the central tower. In one direction, we had a clear view of downtown Los Angeles with its towering and prosperous skyscrapers. When we turned around and looked in the other direction, the street below was a homeless encampment, filled with tents and makeshift shelters. These were the potential

---

1 Eric Resendiz, "Historic Sears Building in Boyle Heights Could Become 'Life Rebuild-ing Center' for Homeless," ABC7, February 19, 2022, https://abc7.com/sears-build-ing-boyle-heights/11578685/#:~:text=%22I%20welcome%20people%20who%20want,-see%20with%20the%20homeless%2C%22%20L.A.

2 Gustavo Arellano, "Column: Can a Giant, Empty Sears Building Help Solve Homelessness in Los Angeles?," *Los Angeles Times,* February 19, 2022, https://www.latimes.com/california/story/2022-02-19/life-rebuilding-center-boyle-heights-sears-building.

residents for the Life Rebuilding Center, and they were crying out for help.

* * *

As part of our effort to win over the city council, Bill and I—along with my son Jonathan—prepared a white paper that outlined in detail the idea behind the Life Rebuilding Center and how we envisioned it impacting the homeless issue. Released in April 2022, it was titled "A Public/Private Partnership for a Long-Term SOLUTION TO HOMELESSNESS for the City and County of Los Angeles."

We defined the three-phase master plan:

1. **PHASE ONE: Immediate Emergency Relief**
   We planned to create a temporary facility at the Sears Building site for immediate use while the main facility was being constructed. My company, the Shomof Group, would house and support approximately two thousand women, men, children, families, veterans, and other vulnerable clients presently living on the streets in nearby Skid Row. Services and assistance would be provided by the Salvation Army, Volunteers of America, Illumination Foundation, and the city and county of Los Angeles, among others.

2. **PHASE TWO: Life Rebuilding Center**
   As we explained in the white paper, "This will be the

largest, most comprehensive Bridge Housing facility ever developed in the United States. . . . The facility will have every imaginable service available on-site, under one roof, to rebuild our clients' lives. This facility will provide real hope and human dignity while becoming a major Community Center asset for the Boyle Heights neighborhood."

3. **PHASE THREE: Permanent Supportive/ Affordable Housing**

   I committed to building thousands of new, afford-able, permanent housing units on the undeveloped nine-acre section that was part of the Sears Building site. These units would be available for those who "graduated" from the six-month Life Rebuilding Center program, giving them a transition back to independent living.

The white paper went into detail about each aspect of the plans, from the medical care and mental health care we would provide, to on-site job training, the safety of residents, and a summary of how the building and overall property would be developed. We even included maps and architectural drawings to provide a real sense of what the entire campus would look like.

From the start, it was always our intention to include members of the community in every decision we made. We encouraged local residents, businesses, and interest groups to become involved, because such a major operation cannot succeed without the support of the people who live in close proximity to it. We were committed to honoring and respecting the opinions and needs of the adjacent Boyle Heights community.

What we planned was a beautification and improvement to the community. We were taking a vacant building and transforming it into something new and exciting that would benefit not just Boyle Heights but also the city of Los Angeles. The Life Rebuilding Center would become known as the ultimate solution for managing homelessness issues in cities of all types and sizes.

Boyle Heights is a community that is only a mile or so from downtown LA. Like many other areas close to downtown, it has seen better days. Unfortunately, some community groups—especially one in particular that met regularly at the Resurrection Church in Boyle Heights—were completely opposed to the Life Rebuilding Center. Their main concern was that such a large concentration of homeless people, many of whom had mental health and substance abuse problems, would add to the crime and drug issues that already plagued the community. They also worried that the area would become overrun with homeless people. Why, they wanted to know, would the city bring thousands of poor people into an area that was already struggling with poverty and crime?

Perhaps the major issue we faced was that people had a preconceived notion of what a facility for the homeless would look like. The typical homeless shelter is dirty and run-down, and the homeless usually hang around on the street near it, day and night, waiting for a meal or a bed. When I explained to protesters that the Life Rebuilding Center was nothing like that—that it would be self-contained with the residents living inside the campus instead of out on the street, and that they would be rehabilitated—most agreed that it was a good idea.

There were also people whose minds could never be changed and who refused to support the project, even after being given all the facts. I met with many groups and individuals who were opposed to the Life Rebuilding Center, and I explained to them that there were already more than a thousand homeless people in Boyle Heights and that another half mile away in the Skid Row area there were an additional five thousand homeless people. My argument to the typical opponent was, "Would you prefer to have all these people on the streets fending for themselves, or have them safely cared for and being rehabilitated in the Life Rebuilding Center?"

Other than the handful of people who were opposed to the project regardless of the facts, it was hard to find anyone who had solid objections to the Life Rebuilding Center once they understood what we hoped to achieve and how we hoped to achieve it. The problem was that the most vocal opponents did not want it in *their* neighborhood under any circumstances. It was a classic "not in my backyard" situation. We attempted to address all their concerns and appease their fears, but it was impossible to change their minds.

This was a classic no-win, "damned if you do, damned

if you don't" dilemma. Years earlier, I was sitting in meetings with a group of community members trying to solve the homeless issue when I brought up the idea of creating shelters in the outskirts of Los Angeles, where land is cheaper. I was yelled at by some community activists who were fighting for the rights of the homeless to be on the streets but had no solutions to the problem. "Why would you want to take them out of Los Angeles?" they said. "These are native Angelenos, and they should stay in Los Angeles. Are you trying to make LA just for the rich?" My answer back to them was, "If I was homeless, I would prefer to be anywhere with a roof over my head than on the streets." The only reason I had proposed this solution was because it would have been too expensive to implement it in the immediate area of downtown LA.

When I proposed doing the same thing in one of my biggest buildings, in the heart of Los Angeles and just half a mile away from Skid Row where the homeless people congregate, it was the same people who were fighting me—except this time they were saying, "Why is it in our backyard?" The truth was, more than a thousand homeless people were in Boyle Heights anyway, and the Life Rebuilding Center would take those who were already there off the streets.

The opponents had no solutions of their own, and it sounded to me as if they were against every solution that was presented to them.

* * *

Because of the opposition to the Life Rebuilding Center in the Boyle Heights neighborhood, the mood in the city council started to sour. Most of the city council members still believed in the project and told me off the record not to lose hope and reassured me that they would still fight for me, but I could definitely sense the change.

That did not stop me from continuing to reach out to the elected officials, including Mayor Eric Garcetti, who still supported the idea. I repeated my main concern, which was that the city and county were not fixing the homeless problem. I had a better solution: take the homeless off the streets and rehabilitate them.

I was particularly focused on Kevin de León, the city council member who represented the district where the Life Rebuilding Center would be located. He ran for mayor of Los Angeles in 2022, and he led me to believe that if he won the election, the Life Rebuilding Center would be one of his top priorities. I'd always respected Kevin and would most likely have backed him for mayor anyway, but this clinched the deal for me. I became a big supporter of his campaign.

In the primary election in June 2022, Kevin came in third behind Karen Bass and Rick Caruso, so he was eliminated from the runoff election in November. I wasn't too concerned because I thought I still had his support in the city council, which was essential. A few weeks later, the community group in Boyle Heights made a lot of headlines with their opposition to my project, and Kevin seemed to be more worried about them as potential voters than as advocates for helping to solve the homeless situation.

In early August, Kevin called me and told me that he was withdrawing his support for the Life Rebuilding Center. I asked him why, and he told me it was because the community was complaining and he was getting pressure from the activists who supported the rights of the homeless to be on the streets.

"Don't let a small minority of the community change your mind," I told him. "This is something that will rebuild people's lives. This is something that will solve the homeless issue."

I also told him that I thought he was making a big mistake. This was the only chance to create the Life Rebuilding Center. I'd already spent millions of dollars and a couple of years of my life on the plan, but I could not keep the building empty for another shot at it in five or ten years with a new set of politicians. I knew of no other building that was as perfectly suited for the Life Rebuilding Center as the Sears Building, where everything could be under one roof—and was available to develop with a willing partner at that moment in history. If I returned to my original idea to convert the building into condominiums with office and retail space, there would be no going back.

Kevin's response stunned me. "I've got a better idea," he said. "Put all the homeless on 747s and fly them to Israel and put them to work on the kibbutzes." I couldn't believe what I'd just heard. Most likely he was joking, but it was a stupid joke that did not go over well, and it was an insult to the homeless. I had already been attacked for wanting to rehabilitate the homeless in the suburbs of Los Angeles, and here was a powerful politician suggesting we move them out of the US altogether.

When I let Kevin know what I thought of his comment, he backtracked. "Izek, I was just kidding," he said. I responded, "Kidding or not, it was a stupid comment." Only a few weeks after this conversation, there was a huge scandal when recordings of Kevin and some other city council members were leaked, revealing them making horribly racist, homophobic, and derogatory remarks. Somehow, I was not surprised to hear this news, and Kevin was unanimously censured by the city council.

The end result was that those who opposed the Life Rebuilding Center had a loud voice, and our elected officials were listening to them more than to reason. That is why it appears that the Life Rebuilding Center is unlikely to see the light of day.

* * *

Meanwhile, the LA Alliance lawsuit against the city and county of Los Angeles, which I discussed in the previous chapter, was still alive. The lawsuit and the Life Rebuilding Center were completely separate issues and had nothing to do with each other, even though they both centered on the city's homeless problem. The lawsuit sought only to force the city and county governments to address the issue of homelessness. The way they were dealing with the homeless was inhumane, allowing them

254

to suffer and die on the streets when there were readily available solutions that were not being used.

On September 12, 2022, the lawsuit was settled in our favor. Under the terms of the agreement, the county committed $236 million to fund services and housing for the most vulnerable people experiencing homelessness—in addition to millions of dollars in state funds and Los Angeles County Measure H funds that were set aside for the homeless. The agreement gave homeless people access to mental health care and substance use disorder services.

In a separate settlement with LA Alliance, the city of Los Angeles agreed to build 10,200 permanent housing units and make 3,100 interim beds available to the homeless. Like homeless shelters, though, this was only a stopgap measure that did nothing to help rehabilitate homeless individuals.

If the Life Rebuilding Center had still been a viable option, it could have provided most of these services and even saved the city a ton of money.

In the election for mayor of Los Angeles in November 2022, I shifted my support to Rick Caruso because he was a businessman who understood how to get things done and he'd assured me that he supported the Life Rebuilding Center. "Help me get elected, and I'll fix the damn problem," he told me. I really thought that the homeless issue could go away if Rick were elected—even without the Life Rebuilding Center—but unfortunately, he lost the election.

The winner, Karen Bass, also told me that she would resolve

the homeless issue, but to me that's the same empty promise that every other politician has to make in order to be elected. Only time will tell whether she is serious and has the political will to use the LA Alliance lawsuit settlement and other resources to finally do something constructive about the situation.

Another development—and the one that may potentially be the final nail in the coffin of the Life Rebuilding Center—was a bizarre decision by the Los Angeles City Council on August 5, 2022. The city council agreed to let the voters decide on a controversial measure that would require all hotels in Los Angeles to make their vacant rooms available to the homeless. The measure, to be voted on in a referendum in 2024, had the backing of some homeless advocacy groups but was opposed by many others, including hotel operators and people like me who cared deeply about the plight of the homeless.

Under the proposed terms, the homeless would be given vouchers for empty rooms, paid for by the city, and the hotels would not be allowed to discriminate against them. I fully support housing the homeless, but this was nothing more than a temporary solution that would negatively affect the hotel business. I can't imagine how many people would be put off by sharing a hotel with the homeless, many of whom have mental health and other issues. The homeless need rehabilitation, not an occasional night in a hotel.

Like all other failed projects, this potential solution would come at a high cost but do absolutely nothing to help the homeless escape from the cycle of homelessness. It would provide no medical care, no job training, and no support. Plus, hotel rooms in Los Angeles are not cheap—averaging considerably more than the $90 to $100 per night that the city would have ended up spending for the Life Rebuilding Center and all of its associated services. If this proposal were to go into effect, the city would be paying premium prices for nothing more than an ill-advised Band-Aid.

The other major problem was that the measure would not be on the ballot for almost two years from the time the city council made their decision. The homeless needed something immediately, which the Life Rebuilding Center could have offered and at a much lower cost.

Despite all these setbacks, I still firmly believe in helping the homeless and finding real solutions to the problem. It may not be the Life Rebuilding Center in the long term, but I will do what I can to make sure I give back to the nation that accepted and opened its arms to me, a hyper kid from Tel Aviv, and to the amazing city that gave me so many opportunities to succeed.

Epilogue

My hobby is collecting classic cars and motorcycles. In the hangar that houses my collection of more than one hundred cars and more than sixty motorcycles, there is a large piece of art hanging on the wall, almost like a mural. It is by a young artist who was one of my tenants and is one of the most amazing artists in Los Angeles. This artwork sums up everything I believe in, and it's one of my most prized possessions. It never ceases to amaze me.

To me, it seems that the artist does not appreciate the United States of America. We certainly don't see eye to eye on every issue, especially because I believe the United States is the greatest country on earth, but there is no doubt about his talent as an artist. He respects me for what I have achieved, and I respect him for his artistic vision and his ability to change the world through art.

He's more "American" than I am, but he doesn't have the same appreciation for the US that I have. He was born here and maybe takes his life and his freedoms for granted—including the freedom to express his dissatisfaction with the United

States—whereas I came here as a fourteen-year-old kid with nothing to my name who was lucky enough to make a life for myself in this beautiful country.

The first artwork of his that I bought is a piece similar to one of his most famous works that was displayed for several months in Pershing Square in downtown Los Angeles, located just a few blocks from my office on Spring. It is about twenty feet high, and it shows a large American flag being fed into a grinder and turned into pennies.

When I offered to buy a smaller version of the artwork, I had one condition: "Take out the pennies," I told him, "and replace them with dollar coins." To him, the piece was a negative statement about commercialization, with the pennies representing peanuts for the masses. I, however, saw it as a representation of the American Dream, with the dollar coins representing prosperity.

He looked at me in a weird way when I asked for the change. "Sure," he responded with a shrug. "I'll do it. I need the money."

At the end of the day, despite his views and his dislike of the system that he believes divides communities and demonizes people for being poor or having different shades of skin, he still had to pay his rent and buy food. In reality, he was a capitalist like me who was in search of his American Dream, and he was happy to sell his artwork to me.

He also made a piece of art specifically for me. He found all these magazine and newspaper articles about me and all the projects I had done to help revitalize the historic downtown area. For the artwork, he combined snippets of all the articles, and at the bottom he added a boy (me) holding a toy car and a girl (Aline) flying balloons. In the background, there is a skyline of all my building projects in the historic downtown. It is a stunning piece of art that shows Izek and Aline living the American Dream. He gave it to me as a gift (although he eventually agreed to accept payment), and I love it. It's hanging in my living room.

The third piece of artwork I purchased is in my garage. It shows the promise of the American Dream, although it also highlights the truth that many people will never get there. The artist meant it as a criticism of the United States, but I see it as being hopeful, because the US is the land of opportunity that gives everyone the chance to make it big.

In the center of this piece, there is what looks like a cheerful advertisement from the 1950s, with the ideal American family—father, mother, two children, and a dog—driving in a new car. A banner above them states, "World's highest standard of living," and a slogan declares, "There's no way like the American Way." To the right is the rich, fat capitalist surrounded by his money, but in contrast to these happy and hopeful images is what looks like a group of poor immigrants who have obviously been left out.

When I first saw this painting in his studio, it reminded me of how far I had come since my childhood in Tel Aviv but also how far the world still has to go to make sure everyone is treated with respect. The artist wanted the rich guy to be seen as someone who doesn't care about the poor, but I saw him as someone actively caring for the poor. Scattered throughout the painting are other images taken from newspaper headlines about the debt crisis, poverty, and the rich-poor divide.

"I know that you created this picture to depict the United States in a negative way," I told him, "but I see positivity in it. I see myself in that picture, because I came here as an immigrant with nothing. I was among those people on the bottom, but I grew up to be one of the people at the top."

My life and my journey from the bottom to the top—from owning my own burger joint at sixteen to making enough money to buy auto shops and then getting into tract homes and high-rise buildings—would not have been possible anywhere except in the United States.

The beauty of the United States of America is that if you work hard, you can become the capitalist sitting on his cash. There is nothing wrong with being that guy—as long as you do it the right way by earning it legally and correctly. The other side of the coin is that if you get there by cheating people or selling drugs or making crooked deals, you're the opposite of a success—you're a failure and a loser, even if you're the richest person in the world. Besides, wealth will not last forever, especially when that wealth has not been earned honestly.

I know many people who have made a lot of money by being dishonest. Just in my own family, there was my cousin Levi, who robbed a bank and made millions as one of the biggest drug lords in the US, and my cousins Etti and Ofer, who were involved in the most notorious bank embezzlement scheme Israel had ever seen. I have never been like my cousins, and I can truthfully say every penny I've made has been earned honestly and legally.

That I saw my story in the artist's image made it important for me to own it, so I paid him a few thousand dollars for the artwork and now it's mine as a reminder of my story. I came from nothing, but I grew up to become a poster boy for the American Way, having an amazing family, traveling the world, and enjoying every minute of living in the United States of America.

The great thing about my story? It is not unique. It has been repeated millions of times in millions of ways. Every person who achieves the American Dream gets there along a different path—but if you play it the right way, you can be both happy and wealthy.

There are still chapters to be written in my life, but I hope that when I look back in the years ahead, I will be proud of what I have achieved. Every major decision I've made in my life involved choosing to go in one direction or another—the right path or the wrong path. I always chose to do what I considered to be the right thing, even if it wasn't the most popular or profitable decision and even if I saw other people getting ahead by making immoral or questionable choices.

What I have discovered is that if you do the right thing, you're not measured by the height of a building or the prestige of the car you drive or the size of your bank account. What matters is that you can look at yourself every day in the mirror and know that you feel good because everything you have done is legitimate. People respect you for that. And once you've achieved your own success, it is also important to do good for others and to search for opportunities to help those—especially our neighbors, friends, and family—who are less fortunate.

Doing the right thing makes you a success. Not everyone can have the same outcome that I've enjoyed, but success is measured in different ways. My father was not financially successful in the same way that I have been, but without exception he did the right thing. He didn't have much money—yet he was the wealthiest person I have known because he was honest and modeled how to live a happy and productive life. The measure of wealth does not necessarily make a person happy. The person who is satisfied with himself and the good deeds he has done is a truly wealthy person.

Like my father, I have tried to live my life well and to be sincere. In the end, I feel good about who I am. It wasn't always easy or straightforward, but I picked the right path, and I am living proof that the American Dream exists.

Acknowledgments

With profound love and appreciation, I take this moment to acknowledge those who have been pillars of support in my life.

My wife, Aline. I could not imagine a life without you. Thank you for being such an amazing wife, mother, and best friend. Like I have always said, I will always support you and be by your side.

My late mother and father, Sara and Hanan. May God rest their souls. You have always been by my side since day one, and without your support, I would have never been able to get where I am today.

My brothers and sisters: Jacob, Sephora, Abe, Malca, Deborah, Mijil, and Aetan. Thank you for being so caring and loving.

My five children and their spouses: Eric and his wife, Jane; Sara;

ACKNOWLEDGMENTS

Jonathan and his wife, Tracy; Jessica and her husband, Aviv; and Jimmy. Thank you for being good, kind, generous, and hardworking people. I will always be proud of you all. And to all twelve of my grandchildren, thank you for making my life so bright and joyful. I cannot wait to see what you all accomplish. I also want to thank my amazing office staff. None of my projects, big or small, would have happened without the hard work all of you put in daily. Thank you. My journey would not be the same without the thousands of people with whom I have worked since I was sixteen. From my lawyers, architects, engineers, consultants, brokers, contractors, and all our property managers—nothing would have been accomplished without your dedication.

Last but certainly not least, I want to thank the next generation of dreamers, entrepreneurs, and visionaries. This book is for you. It was crafted in a way that hopefully inspires you to work hard, with integrity and kindness to achieve greatness. If my story can play a small part in your life, I hope you find great inspiration and motivation to go after your dreams and make a positive impact in this world. And always remember, dreams don't die . . .

Best,
Izek Shomof